The Stigmatized Vernacular

ENCOUNTERS: Explorations in Folklore and Ethnomusicology
Michael Dylan Foster and Ray Cashman, Editors

A *Journal of Folklore Research* Book

The Stigmatized Vernacular

Where Reflexivity Meets Untellability

Edited by Diane E. Goldstein and Amy Shuman

INDIANA UNIVERSITY PRESS

Bloomington and Indianapolis

This book is a publication of

Indiana University Press
Office of Scholarly Publishing
Herman B Wells Library 350
1320 East 10th Street
Bloomington, Indiana 47405 USA

iupress.indiana.edu

The paper used in this publication meets the minimum requirements of the American National Standard for Information Sciences—Permanence of Paper for Printed Library Materials, ANSI Z39.48–1992.

Manufactured in the United States of America

Catalog information is available from the Library of Congress.

ISBN 978-0-253-02440-4 (pbk.)
ISBN 978-0-253-02443-5 (ebk.)

DOI: 10.2979/stigmatizedvernacular.0.0.00

1 2 3 4 5   21 20 19 18 17 16

Contents

The Stigmatized Vernacular

Diane E. Goldstein and Amy Shuman

The Stigmatized Vernacular: Where Reflexivity Meets Untellability

IN A MOVING and now classic 1989 reconsideration of his earlier work on the Ilongot headhunters of Luzon, Philippines, anthropologist Renato Rosaldo described his inability to grasp the rage that would compel someone to cut off a human head. The Ilongot spoke of severing and tossing a victim's head away as an act that enabled the headhunter to discard the anger that arises from bereavement. In "Grief and a Headhunter's Rage," Rosaldo wrote of his inability to understand grief and anger so powerful that it would lead to such brutal action—until he experienced the sudden tragic loss of his wife Michelle in 1981, when during a fieldwork trip in the Philippines she lost her footing and fell to her death. Rosaldo characterizes his journal entries following Michelle's death by saying they "reflect more broadly on death and rage and headhunting by speaking of my 'wish for the Ilongot solution'" (1993, 11). He continues, "They are much more in touch with reality than Christians" (11). In a subsequent reflection, Rosaldo notes:

> One burden of this introduction concerns the claim that it took some fourteen years for me to grasp what Ilongots had told me about grief, rage, and headhunting. During all those years I was not yet in a position to comprehend the force of anger possible in bereavement, and now I am. Introducing myself into this account requires a certain hesitation both because of the discipline's taboo and because of its increasingly frequent violation by essays laced with trendy amalgams of continental philosophy and autobiographical snippets. (2004, 170)

Rosaldo's words render visible the deep connections among stigma, cultural vernaculars, the position of researchers, and the untellable, unwriteable, and unspeakable. Conducting research on a stigmatized, brutally violent cultural act (understood differently by those who engage in its performance), studying that performance from a position of distance and then from a position too close, Rosaldo makes tellable things that resist representation, resist reading, and resist hearing. He recognizes the stigma of his own act of understanding and making visible, in a deep and close way, the motives of those labeled as *barbaric*, motives and samenesses preferred invisible in the face of desired difference and distance. Rosaldo's newfound reflexive understanding of angry horrific brutality in fact engages a double stigma, one for the act practiced by the Ilongot, and another for his own ability to understand and perhaps even sympathize. Rosaldo's piece was risky, putting words (and empathetic words at that) to an act so heinous that to say it is stigmatized seems wrong, that is, the labeling, the othering, and the distancing appear self-evident. Furthermore, Rosaldo broke the "us" and "them" barrier, and, as could be expected, was amply criticized for doing so.[1]

Over the last five years a number of linked panels at the American Folklore Society Meetings have been organized under the title "The Stigmatized Vernacular." This effort has explored double stigmas: those situations where not only are individuals stigmatized but so are the vernaculars associated with them. As part of this multi-layered conversation about stigma, this book discusses the relationship between the stigmatized individual and our role as researchers. We address our own perspectives as researchers struggling with stigma issues and tellability, as well as scholarly reflexive concerns dealing with what *can't* be said when working with stigmatized groups or topics.

This work builds on Erving Goffman's concept of stigma and the management of spoiled identities (1963); on Harvey Sacks's (1992) and William Labov's (1967) notions of tellability and its counterpart, untellability; and on decades of work on reflexivity and political representation. It builds also on Amy Shuman's notion that stigma is a form of hypervisibility that obscures other experiences and on Diane Goldstein's (2009) work on the vernacular politics of narrative. Focusing on stigma, the chapters in this volume discuss the institutional constraints researchers faced during the fieldwork and writing processes; authors explore issues of reflexivity, representation, and 'stigma veneration' as they emerged during research on type 2 diabetes, accounts of tobacco farming, the sometimes chaotic untellable narratives of trauma, and the quest for political asylum.

All four chapters demonstrate how folklore research contributes to understanding the cultural politics of stigma, that is, not only what is stigmatized by different groups, but also which resources people employ to manage the discrimination, prejudice, or oppression that can result from stigma. Goffman distinguished between the discredited, that is, individuals recognized as belonging (sometimes by association only) to a stigmatized group, and the discreditable, that is, individuals who are vulnerable to stigmatization. *Discreditable* is an especially interesting cultural category because it implies the possibility that someone can 'pass' as long as his or her stigma is not recognized or revealed; in this sense, stigma can involve a process of discovery. The maintenance of such a category involves processes of surveillance, often by informal gatekeepers.

The Stigmatized Vernacular

Goffman's foundational work *Stigma: Notes on the Management of Spoiled Identity* (1963) has inspired nearly five decades of elaboration and ethnographic illustration of stigma's negative impact in the lives of individuals affected by everything from unemployment and marginalized occupations to race and religion, disease and disability, sexual practice and sexual orientation. Over the years, notions of stigma have varied somewhat from Goffman's definition; he saw stigma as an attribute that is "deeply discrediting" and that reduces the bearer "from a whole and usual person to a tainted, discounted one" (3). As social science writing on stigma has developed over the years, it has been most elaborated in the field of social psychology by researchers who have focused predominantly on the construction of stigma-related cognitive categories (Link and Phelan 2001). One of the significant critiques of these studies is that they tend to be uninformed by the lived experience of those who find themselves affected by stigma. In writing about epilepsy, for example, Joseph Schneider argues that most able-bodied experts give priority to "scientific theories and research techniques rather than to the words and perceptions of the people they study" (1988, 64).

Such a comment is a call to arms for folklorists, entrenched as we are in the words and experiences of the people with whom we work.

Our disciplinary focus positions us well to concentrate on the vernacular experience of the stigmatized, but it also propels us toward analysis of the performance of stigma, the process of stigmatization, and the political representation of stigmatized populations. These perspectives come to the fore in the chapters that follow, as does the multi-layered nature of stigma—its ability to reproduce, overlap, and spread, not just in terms of replication, but also in terms of the ethnographer's ability to apprehend it and her ability to research and write about it. The phrase *the stigmatized vernacular* is intended to capture not only the emic experience of stigmatization, but also the contagion of stigma—the way it spills over beyond the topic into the means of articulation.

Unlike some of the other terms used for folklore—for example, *popular antiquities* or *local cultural productions*—the term *vernacular* carries with it the possibility of stigma, as, for example, when that term is used to describe a non-standard language. Dell Hymes argued vehemently against the stigma attached to non-standard languages and for recognition of what he called language equality, especially the value of the vernacular (1992, 1). Henry Glassie goes further in his attempts to valorize the vernacular:

> [W]e call buildings "vernacular" because they embody values alien to those cherished in the academy. When we called buildings "folk," the implication was that they countered in commonness and tradition the pretense and progress that dominate simple academic schemes.... The study of vernacular architecture, through its urge toward the comprehensive, accommodates cultural diversity. It welcomes the neglected into study in order to acknowledge the reality of difference and conflict. (2000, 20)

For both Hymes and Glassie, the vernacular references diversity; both scholars promote the vernacular as part of a critique of the stigma of difference. Not all vernaculars are stigmatized, and not all stigmatizing practices are directed at the ordinary, everyday, or folk (to suggest some apparently synonymous concepts). Rather than point to word origins—a move that can claim a deceptive empiricism if the history of a word's unfolding meanings is ignored—we are interested in the kinds of contrasts the term *vernacular* has served. The Latin *vernaculum* distinguished between the "homebred, homespun, homegrown, homemade" and "things obtained in formal exchange. The child of one's slave and of one's wife, the donkey born of one's own beast, were vernacular beings, as was the staple that came from the gardens or commons" (Illich 1980, 85).

In folklore research, the concept of the vernacular has been applied not only to language and architecture, but also to music. Thus the vernacular is interestingly contrasted with the term *creole*, which originally designated a European born in Latin America (Cara 2003). Unlike *creole*, which describes the emergence of new, combined, musical forms (as well as cultural practices and people), *vernacular* can imply a claim to indigeneity. For the most part, at least when used by Hymes and Glassie, *vernacular* was intended to replace other, more stigmatizing terms and phrases, such as *low culture, primitive*, or even *folk* itself. In suggesting the category of 'stigmatized vernacular,' we intend to open up questions regarding indigeneity, cultural/racial mixing, high and low, expert and lay knowledge—contested conceptualizations that we suggest are central to folkloristics.

The stigmatized vernacular is dialectically associated with the venerated vernacular. Several scholars have offered accounts of how the vernacular becomes associated with the stigmatized. Ivan Illich (1980) argues that every attempt to substitute a universal commodity for a vernacular value has led not to equality, but to a hierarchical modernization of poverty. Cindy Patton (1992) argues that the appropriation of vernaculars always ends in embarrassment because the appropriator never knows all the rules for usage and the new context never fits exactly. James C. Scott (2009) describes borrowed, appropriated, and commodified vernaculars—that is, vernaculars detached from context—as "vernaculars cross-dressing or dressed up to travel." Each theorist proposes that value gets reconfigured when things are taken out of context. These observations are a good starting point for considering the relationship between vernacularity and value. However, they assume a point 'before' things are borrowed or taken out of context, and by implication also assume that visibility/tellability are less disturbed (or not disturbed at all) in this previous moment.

We suggest that folkloristics, the field most engaged with the positive values of the vernacular, is in a good position to rethink the relationship between stigma and vernacularity. The chapters that follow consider several possible configurations of stigma and vernacular. Ann Ferrell considers the stigmatized vernacular in relation to discourses of heritage. She discusses how some narratives about tobacco farming are more tellable than others in particular contexts, especially outside the context of the farmers' own discussions. She points out that the economic and symbolic discourses about tobacco have been discursively separated, such that, for example, tobacco as heritage becomes less stigmatized in comparison to tobacco growing as an ongoing way of life. To some extent, then, stigma erases one vernacular in favor of another.

Whereas Ferrell's discussion of stigmatized tobacco farmers describes a vernacular practice that has changed in value to outsiders, Sheila Bock discusses how the stigma associated with type 2 diabetes is enacted, rejected, and/or promoted in everyday (vernacular) conversations and performances of self. As she demonstrates, vernacular cultural discourses keep stigmas in place. Here the vernacular can be aligned with the ordinary knowledge of people in their everyday lives in contrast to medical knowledge. It is fascinating to consider how medical and vernacular discourses both intersect and compete for meaning.

Diane Goldstein explores the representational politics surrounding untellability and stigma, especially in those situations in which trauma or mental and physical challenges result in 'chaotic narratives' that only serve to further stigmatize individuals. Goldstein focuses on the experience, the content, and the context of traumatic untellability in order to re-examine issues related to scholarly choices of speaking for, about, or without.

Amy Shuman and Carol Bohmer describe political asylum applicants as caught between discourses of veneration (that honor survivors of horrible situations) and discourses of repudiation (that regard applicants through a lens of suspicion). The narratives told by asylum seekers articulate one form of the stigmatized vernacular. Shuman and Bohmer discuss how vastly different, unfamiliar, and terrifying situations are multiply stigmatized as not only barbaric but also as not-credible, as beyond the pale of the possible, as hypervisible but not recognizable. They, like the other authors of this volume, suggest an important link between the stigmatized vernacular and the tellable (and recognizable).

Tellability, the Untellable, and Reflexivity

The notion of tellability comes to us from the important narrative writings of William Labov (1972) and Harvey Sacks ([1974] 1989,

1992). Later joined by Livya Polanyi (1979), Shuman (1986), Monika Fludernik (1996), Elinor Ochs and Lisa Capps (2001), Neal Norrick (2005), and others, Labov and Sacks argued that reportability or tell-ability is *the* crucial requirement for competent narration. It is what allows a narrator to defend his or her story as relevant and newsworthy—to get and hold the floor and escape censure at its conclusion (Polanyi 1981). Tellability addresses audience expectations, newsworthiness, uniqueness, relevance, importance, and humor but also—and perhaps just as centrally—appropriateness, contextualization, negotiation, mediation, and entitlement. As Labov notes, there is no absolute standard of inherent tellability—in appropriate circumstances, even that which is trite or commonplace can be told with power and affect. But the reverse is also true. As Norrick writes,

> Tellers do not report just any accident; they report "the most gosh awful wreck" they have ever seen, as in Sacks' story "Down to Ventura." Such claims for tellability typically appear in the preface to a story, and tellers typically come back to the newsworthiness at the end, picking up a phrase from the preface, which refers to the news at its beginning: "It wasn't in the paper last night. I looked." A story about "the most gosh-awful wreck on the Ventura Freeway" may be tellable as news, but at some point the gruesome details of the wreck with the dead and injured, the blood and guts goes beyond the tellable into areas of the no longer tellable. (2005, 324)

Donna Wyckoff (1996), Elaine Lawless (2001), Shuman (1986, 2006), Goldstein (2009), Shuman and Carol Bohmer (2004), and others have explored the nature of untellable narratives in the context of sexual abuse, violence, and political unrest, and similar notions of narrative management in the face of social stigma have been discussed by David Hufford (1976), Lauri Honko (1964), Christine Cartwright (1982), Gillian Bennett (1987), and Goldstein (1991) in relation to the expression of personal supernatural experiences. These works focus on the kinds of experiences that can or cannot be talked about in particular contexts, the factors that limit such narrating, and the risk-taking inherent in the telling of certain types of personal narratives. Stories become untellable because the content defies articulation, the rules of appropriateness outweigh the import of content, the narrator is constrained by issues of entitlement and storytelling rights, or the space the narratives would normally inhabit is understood by the narrator as somehow unsafe. Narrative telling can be risky business, not just in terms of the personal discursive risk for the tale teller, but also as narration reflects on, and acts upon, others potentially implicated in narrative events.

In particular, untellable narratives are connected to what bell hooks describes as questions about who is "worthy to speak and be heard" (1992, 176). As many scholars have noted, narrative is one means for individuals to negotiate and produce identities, sometimes in relation to otherwise stigmatizing characterizations (Bamberg 1997; Georgakopoulou 2002; Mishler 2006). Narrators align themselves, the characters in the taleworld, and the storyrealm (Young 1987) in order to produce a particular stance. Along these lines, Bamberg's three elements of positioning (how characters are positioned in relation to events, in relation to the audience, and in relation to themselves) could be applied to stigma—for example, to consider how particular practices or events are stigmatized, how narrative is used to persuade listeners to accept or reject particular characters and their practices, and how people describe themselves and others—whether as protagonist or antagonist, blameworthy or innocent, or credible or disbelieved (1997, 337). The negotiation of what is tellable or untellable relies in part on these alignments. As Harold Garfinkel has observed, stigma and its opposite—that which is considered 'normal'—always invoke a relationship between the tellable and the untellable ([1967] 1984, 181).

Stigma as Hypervisibility

Goffman's work on stigma explored the multiple possibilities and consequences of visibility, invisibility, tellability, untellability, passing, and being exposed/exposing oneself. He dismantled the binaries of tellable/untellable or visible/invisible by demonstrating that these categories are situational and interactive. Visibility is produced by interactions in which semiotic codes enable saliency, that is, identify particular features as marked. The categories of marked and unmarked can be relatively value-neutral in language and can be used to point out differences that are not necessarily accompanied by stigma. For example, *tea*, the unmarked variety, can refer to sweetened ice tea in South Carolina and unsweetened hot tea in Boston. As Frantz Fanon argued, the category 'white' is anything but neutral, and in purporting to be an unmarked category, it stigmatizes the marked, 'black' skin (see

Silverman 1996). Kaja Silverman argues, "The black subject described by Fanon is not only in 'combat' with the image through which he is 'photographed' by the seemingly white gaze but is also irresistibly drawn to the 'mirror' of an ideal 'whiteness'" (1996, 29). In more recent work, Georgios Anagnostu discusses the role of whiteness in the use of the category 'model minority,' a category that offers the removal of stigma to those few who get a high grade on what Micaela di Leonardo (1998, 70) calls an "ethnic report card: the positive valuation and public flaunting of those traits that are seen as leading to mobility" (Anagnostu 2009, 9).

The "public flaunting" of cultural practices, whether by a group itself or by others who appropriate and recontextualize practices, creates hypervisibility in contrast but always connected to invisibility. Invisibility and hypervisibility both reference asymmetrical power relations. For example, Charles Briggs and Clara Mantini-Briggs discuss how the visibility/invisibility/hypervisibility of cholera participates in other asymmetries, in which two groups (in their case, creole and indigenous groups) are represented as separate but equal, but the discourse is actually "a cover for asymmetrical relationships, where one group is constructed as the complete version and the other is a partial and defective copy" (2003, 251). (An alternative reading is that one group is authentic and the other is inauthentic.)

In other words, stigma often depends on discourses that explicitly promote difference and implicitly contain hierarchies of value. Authenticity is one of those discourses, providing value but often at the cost of stigma. Notably, Theodor Adorno suggested, "[A]nything that does not wish to wither should rather take on itself the stigma of the inauthentic" (in Jay 2006, 22). Along those lines, folkloristics has had a paradigm shift in recent decades, from an effort to find the authentic folk to an interest in identifying the conditions in which authenticity is produced (Bendix 1997; Kirshenblatt-Gimblett 1998). Folklorists today recognize the field's earlier preoccupation with finding the unmarked, untarnished folk actually marked those people as exotic others. Today, in explorations of heritage culture (e.g., Ferrell, this volume), folklorists explore what it might mean to take on "the stigma of the inauthentic." That process of inquiry begins by asking how cultural practices are valued and disvalued, which dimensions of humanity are unmarked and which are marked.

A next step would be to ask about the necessity of the relationship between visibility/invisibility and tellability/untellability. Goffman's work calls attention to the relationship between visibility and tellability without arguing that they are inextricably linked. For example, he undertakes elaborate inquiries about both stigma and alignment, but he does not connect the two issues. He considers stigma as a problem of tellability/untellability, and he considers how speakers take up a particular alignment, or stance, with regard to each other, but he does not consider how alignment might produce, resist, enable, or confront stigma. In the chapters in this volume, we ask whether or not we should, as Peggy Phelan suggests, take "as axiomatic the link between the image and the word, that what one can see is in every way related to what one can say" (1993, 2).

The chapters in this volume also take into consideration methodological issues of fieldwork, especially the problem of accurately representing contingent truths. Václav Havel wrote that truth "is not simply what you think it is; it is also the circumstances in which it is said, and to whom, why, and how it is said" (1990, 67). This does not mean that the truth is up for grabs, but rather that it must be pinned down, and it does not remain pinned down but rather requires constant attention to context. This fundamental premise of the ethnography of communication as conceived by Dell Hymes has particular resonance for considering not just the varieties (vernacularity) of everyday communication and performance, but also how stigma is produced by the constraints of what gets told, by whom, to whom, and about whom.

In writing about the stigmatized vernacular, the authors of these essays have considered those constraints not only as objects of study, but also as questions of ethics and methodology. In each essay, the people discussed are included in the intended audience; further, each author is in conversation with the relevant policymakers, lawyers, public health professionals, and advocates. If the language of the essays isn't entirely familiar to folklorists, that may be because we see our task as opening a conversation broader than the discipline. We hope to be making a contribution to folkloristics, but we are not claiming that this conversation belongs only to us.

To return to Rosaldo's example, we are reminded that although our goal may be mutual understanding, and although our project might be an effort to understand how gaps in understanding stigmatized vernaculars occur, not all understandings are tellable without cost. Although untellability has begun to be explored in narrative research, it has not generally been applied to our thinking about reflexive or auto-ethnography—to the storytelling rights of ethnographers, the things we see, experiences that defy articulation, our unsafe spaces. Our effort, in the pages that follow, is to unpack the interstitial gaps that form in the representational narratives surrounding stigma, and, like Rosaldo, to venture into those spaces of silence and identify the conditions in which speaking is or is not possible.

Note

1. See, for example, critiques discussed by Ruth Behar, including the argument that "Michelle's death gave Renato a new-found sense of ethnographic authority, a sense that he is capable of feeling everything the Ilongot do" (1996, 171).

References

Anagnostu, Georgios. 2009. *Contours of White Ethnicity: Popular Ethnography and the Making of Usable Pasts in Greek America.* Athens: Ohio University Press.

Bamberg, Michael G. W. 1997. "Positioning Between Structure and Performance." *Journal of Narrative and Life History* 7 (1–4): 335–62.

Behar, Ruth. 1996. *The Vulnerable Observer: Anthropology that Breaks Your Heart.* Boston: Beacon Press.

Bendix, Regina. 1997. *In Search of Authenticity: The Formation of Folklore Studies.* Madison: University of Wisconsin Press.

Bennett, Gillian. 1987. *Traditions of Belief: Women, Folklore and the Supernatural Today.* London: Pelican Books.

Briggs, Charles, and Clara Mantini-Briggs. 2003. *Stories in a Time of Cholera: Racial Profiling during a Medical Nightmare.* Berkeley and Los Angeles: University of California Press.

Cara, Ana. 2003. "The Poetics of Creole Talk: Toward an Aesthetic of Argentine Verbal Art." *Journal of American Folklore* 116 (459): 36–56.

Cartwright, Christine A. 1982. " 'To the Saints Which are at Ephesus . . .': A Case Study in the Analysis of Religious Memorates." *New York Folklore Quarterly* 8:57–71.

Di Leonardo, Micaela. 1998. *Exotics at Home: Anthropologies, Others, American Modernity.* Chicago: University of Chicago Press.

Fludernik, Monika. 1996. *Towards a "Natural" Narratology.* London: Routledge.

Garfinkel, Harold. (1967) 1984. *Studies in Ethnomethodology.* Malden, MA: Blackwell Publishers. First published by Prentice-Hall.

Georgakopoulou, Alexandra. 2002. "Narrative and Identity Management: Discourse and Social Identities in a Tale of Tomorrow." *Research on Language and Social Interaction* 35:427–51.

Glassie, Henry. 2000. *Vernacular Architecture*. Bloomington: Indiana University Press.

Goffman, Erving. 1963. *Stigma: Notes on the Management of Spoiled Identity*. Englewood Cliffs, NJ: Prentice Hall.

Goldstein, Diane E. 1991. "Perspectives on Newfoundland Belief Traditions: Narrative Clues to Concepts of Evidence." In *Studies in Newfoundland Folklore: Community and Process*, edited by G. Thomas and J. D. A. Widdowson, 27–40. St. John's, Newfoundland: Breakwater Books.

———. 2009. "The Sounds of Silence: Foreknowledge, Miracles, Suppressed Narratives, and Terrorism—What Not Telling Might Tell Us." *Western Folklore* 68 (3): 235–57.

Havel, Václav. 1990. *Disturbing the Peace: A Conversation with Karel Hvíž'ala*. London: Faber & Faber.

Honko, Lauri. 1964. "Memorates and the Study of Folk Beliefs." *Journal of the Folklore Institute* 1 (1): 5–19.

hooks, bell. 1992. *Black Looks: Race and Representation*. Boston, MA: South End Press.

Hufford, David. 1976. "Ambiguity and the Rhetoric of Belief." *Keystone Folklore Quarterly* 21:11–24.

Hymes, Dell. 1992. "Inequality in Language: Taking for Granted." *Working Papers in Educational Linguistics* 8 (1): 1–30.

Illich, Ivan. 1980. "Vernacular Values." *Philosophica* 26 (2): 47–102. Online at http://logica.ugent.be/philosophica/fulltexts/26-3.pdf.

Jay, Martin. 2006. "Taking on the Stigma of Inauthenticity: Adorno's Critique of Genuineness." *New German Critique* 97 (333): 15–30.

Kirshenblatt-Gimblett, Barbara. 1998. *Destination Culture: Tourism, Museums, and Heritage*. Berkeley and Los Angeles: University of California Press.

Labov, William. 1972. *Language in the Inner City*. Philadelphia: University of Pennsylvania Press.

Labov, William, and Joshua Waletzky. 1967. "Narrative Analysis: Oral Versions of Personal Experience." In *Essays on the Verbal and Visual Arts*, edited by June L. Helm, 12–44. Seattle: University of Washington Press.

Lantis, Margaret. 1960. "Vernacular Culture." *American Anthropologist* 62 (2): 202–16.

Lawless, Elaine J. 2001. *Women Escaping Violence: Empowerment through Narrative*. Columbia: University of Missouri Press.

Link, Bruce G., and Jo C. Phelan. 2001. "Conceptualizing Stigma." *Annual Review of Sociology* 27:363–85.

Mishler, Elliot G. 2006. Narrative and Identity: The Double Arrow of Time. In *Discourse and Identity*, edited by A. de Fina, D. Schiffrin, and M. Bamberg, 30–47. Studies in Interactional Sociolinguistics 23. Cambridge: Cambridge University Press.

Norrick, Neal R. 2005. "The Dark Side of Tellability." *Narrative Inquiry* 15 (2): 323–43.

Ochs, Elinor, and Lisa Capps. 2001. *Living Narrative: Creating Lives in Everyday Storytelling*. Cambridge, MA: Harvard University Press.

———. 1996. "Narrating the Self." *Annual Review of Anthropology* 25:19–43.

Patton, Cindy. 1992. "Designing Safer Sex: Pornography as Vernacular." In *A Leap in the Dark: AIDS, Art & Contemporary Cultures*, edited by Allan Klusa¥ek and Ken Morrison, 192–206. Montreal: Véhicule Press.

Phelan, Peggy. 1993. *Unmarked: The Politics of Performance.* London: Routledge.

Polanyi, Livia. 1979. "So What's the Point?" *Semiotica* 25:207–41.

———. 1981. "What Stories Can Tell Us about Their Teller's World." *Poetics Today* 2 (2): 97–112.

Rosaldo, Renato. (1989) 1993. "Grief and a Headhunter's Rage." In *Culture and Truth: The Remaking of Social Analysis*, 1–21. Boston: Beacon Press.

———. 2004. "Grief and a Headhunter's Rage." In *Death, Mourning and Burial: A Cross Cultural Reader*, edited by Antonius C. G. M. Robben, 167–78. Oxford: Blackwell.

Sacks, Harvey. (1974) 1989. "An Analysis of the Course of a Joke's Telling." In *Explorations in the Ethnography of Speaking*, edited by Richard Bauman and Joel Sherzer, 337–53. 2nd ed. Studies in the Social and Cultural Foundations of Language 8. Cambridge: Cambridge University Press.

———. 1992. *Lectures on Conversation*, vols. 1 and 2. Edited by Gail Jefferson. Oxford: Blackwell.

Schneider, Joseph W. 1988. "Disability as Moral Experience: Epilepsy and Self in Routine Relationships." *Journal of Social Issues* 44 (1): 63–78.

Scott, James C. 2009. "Vernaculars Cross-Dressed as Universals: Globalization as North Atlantic Hegemony." *Macalester International* 24 (1): 7.

Shuman, Amy. 1986. *Storytelling Rights: The Uses of Oral and Written Texts by Urban Adolescents.* Cambridge: Cambridge University Press.

———. 2006. "Entitlement and Empathy in Personal Narrative." *Narrative Inquiry* 16 (1): 148–55.

Shuman, Amy and Carol Bohmer. 2004. "Representing Trauma: Political Asylum Narrative." *Journal of American Folklore* 117 (466): 394–14.

Silverman, Kaja. 1996. *The Threshold of the Visible World.* New York: Routledge.

Wyckoff, Donna. 1996. "'Now Everything Makes Sense!': Complicating the Contemporary Legend Picture." In *Contemporary Legend: A Reader*, edited by Gillian Bennett and Paul Smith, 363–80. New York: Garland.

Young, Katharine Galloway. 1987. *Taleworlds and Storyrealms: The Phenomenology of Narrative.* Martinus Nijhoff Philosophy Library 16. The Hague: Martinus Nijhoff.

DIANE E. GOLDSTEIN is Professor and former Chair of the Department of Folklore and Ethnomusicology at Indiana University and formerly served as President of the American Folklore Society in 2012–2013. Her publications include *Talking AIDS: Interdisciplinary Perspectives on Acquired Immune Deficiency Syndrome, Once Upon a Virus: AIDS Legends and Vernacular Risk Perception* and *Haunting Experiences: Ghosts in Contemporary Folklore.*

AMY SHUMAN is Professor of Folklore at The Ohio State University. Her publications include *Storytelling Rights: The Uses of Oral and Written Texts by Urban Adolescents* (2006), *Other People's Stories: Entitlement Claims and the Critique of Empathy* (2010), and, with Carol Bohmer, *Rejecting Refugees: Political Asylum in the 21st Century* (2008).

1 "It's Really Hard to Tell the True Story of Tobacco": Stigma, Tellability, and Reflexive Scholarship

DURING MY TIME as an American Association of University Women (AAUW) fellow in 2008–2009, I was asked to speak to a Vermont AAUW chapter about my research on Kentucky burley tobacco farming.[1] I began my talk this way:

> Imagine that you are a fifth-generation farmer of a farm product that is now in less demand. Much of it is being imported from overseas, and the product is associated with illness and death. . . . Now imagine that product is milk. What would that mean in Vermont?[2]

I thought for a long time about how to open my talk to this Vermont audience. Based on the responses and reactions that I had previously experienced when I talked about my research, I knew that their ideas about tobacco were probably based in particular stories that have contributed to the construction of a dominant and publicly acceptable way of speaking about tobacco. I wanted to acknowledge these 'tellable' narratives—and couch tobacco farming in other, more locally (and publicly) resonant discourses—so that my audience would be willing to hear about my research.

In this chapter, I describe how I came to examine assumptions about tobacco production and tobacco producers—both my own assumptions and those of others that I encountered—in order to discover what was deemed tellable in public discourses. A number of scholars have explored the idea of tellability, most often with regard to personal narratives and small-scale interactions. For instance, in their classic 1967 study William Labov and Joshua Waletzky describe "evaluation" as necessary to successful personal narratives: the narrator's evaluative moves work to explain why he or she finds the story reportable in a particular context. That is, they establish tellability. And within the context of conversation analysis, Harvey Sacks argues that *listeners* monitor whether a narrative has value—whether it is "'tellable' in the sense of 'worth telling'" (1967, 776). Amy Shuman (2005) and Diane Goldstein (2009) build on these concepts in their work on personal experience narratives and legend, and both suggest that the reverse situation, *un*tellability, is important as well.[3] Though much work on tellability and untellability centers on stories told by individual narrators, in this chapter I suggest that these concepts can be applied as productively to public discourses—talk (oral and written, vernacular and institutional) about the topic in the public sphere that reflects common, but often unquestioned, ideas and assumptions. As I will describe, the shifting public discourses about tobacco products and the tobacco industry influence talk about tobacco farming, and this interaction helps to determine what is and is not tellable. Although tobacco farmers themselves often rely on the tellable narratives I will describe, they made it clear to me that other, less familiar narratives are central to understanding the changing contexts of this traditional cultural practice—a practice that is first and foremost an occupation.

In describing how I came to locate both tellable and untellable narratives, I also suggest that increased reflexivity in our scholarship means expanding our ideas about what counts as data. For instance, I have found it useful to take note of my own personal and disciplinary assumptions and to draw on a range of informal and publicly mediated conversations about tobacco. As my interest grew to include the emerging and evolving discourses surrounding tobacco farming in the context of other public discourses on tobacco, I moved beyond the ethnographic data I had expected to collect and began to also examine data from oral, print, and internet sources, both past and present. This data is certainly not unconventional; the data that brought me to it, however, is. As I describe, it was data that I gathered beyond the field— from outsiders to the tradition I was researching—that led me to expand my research in order to understand what has become tellable.

Fieldwork Beyond the Field

The transitional circumstances facing contemporary tobacco farmers call out for documentation and interpretation, and so I began my fieldwork with a fairly conventional folklore project in mind. In 2005, Kentucky tobacco farmers were facing the end of the federal tobacco program that had been in place since the 1930s: for the first time in seventy years, they would have to raise tobacco without quotas and price supports.[4] In addition, demand for their crop has continued to decline, not only because of what seems most obvious—declining tobacco use—but also because of the changing purchasing habits of tobacco manufacturers. For instance, between 1970 and 2002, burley tobacco imported into the United States for domestic use grew from .6 percent to 48.1 percent (Capehart 2007). Like other farmers, tobacco producers also face changing technologies, rising input costs, stagnant or falling sale prices, labor shortages, and pressures to expand and/or diversify their operations. For these and other reasons, many farmers have stopped raising tobacco altogether.

As I set out into the field, my research trajectory seemed fairly straightforward. After all, tobacco farming is a centuries-old family and occupational tradition, and the current decline has major implications for individual farmers, as well as for tobacco communities and regions.[5] But fieldwork is a process of recognizing and responding to assumptions, particularly when they are challenged. My experience was no different: over the course of my fieldwork most of my assumptions were called into question. One of my central assumptions—the idea that there were very few tobacco farmers left in Kentucky—had itself been shaped by public discourses. Another key assumption that I had not recognized was challenged both in the field and out of it—namely, the idea that I could study tobacco farming as a cultural practice without considering the use of tobacco products, the health effects of tobacco use, and the actions of tobacco product manufacturers. I came to learn that tobacco farmers must adapt to more than marketing- and production-centered changes; they also face changes in the social and political status of the crop they grow.

In casual conversations with family, friends, and even mere acquaintances, my attempts to answer the inevitable question "What's your research about?" generated a range of responses that required evolving negotiations on my part; gradually, I began to realize that these conversations were important.[6] For instance, a good friend who knew that I had once been a smoker asked me, "Is it hard to not smoke, doing your fieldwork with tobacco farmers?" At the time, the question confused me, since my fieldwork was about tobacco farming, not smoking.

Frequently I am asked, "Do *they* smoke?" Implied is the question, "Do tobacco farmers know/admit that tobacco use is unhealthy?" On a number of occasions I've also been asked how farmers "feel" about raising tobacco—with the suggestion that they should feel *guilty*. These questions suggest a belief that tobacco farmers must be in some sort of collective denial about the health effects of tobacco use; otherwise they surely wouldn't grow it. More than once—and I remember this most vividly in a conversation with two complete strangers at a baby shower—individuals overtly expressed the implications of these more subtle questions: "How can they grow something that kills people?"

Other questions that I encountered expressed surprise that tobacco farming remains viable in contemporary American agriculture. "Do people still grow tobacco?" I was often asked. Sometimes people would remark, "I used to see tobacco growing on my drive from [place A] to [place B]. It's so sad that it's gone now." Often, people shared stories that they had heard in the news about farmers abandoning tobacco for organic vegetables, or about tobacco barns either collapsing in disrepair or being converted to other uses because they were no longer needed.

Responses to my research in academic contexts were important to attend to as well. For instance, in the spring of 2009, I had the opportunity to design and teach a course titled "Tobacco in American Culture" at a small private college in Vermont. As a first-day activity, I asked students to list their associations with the word *tobacco*, and within a short time I had filled an entire board with words and phrases such as *the Marlboro man, Joe Camel*, and *Skoal*; *plantations* and *slaves*; *lung cancer* and *emphysema*; and so on. We then discussed the fact that not a single student had referenced present-day tobacco farmers. The students had never envisioned this group. On another occasion, an article manuscript that I submitted to an American Studies journal was rejected; the editor noted that "the historical study of tobacco and identity raises far-reaching questions about the political economy of tobacco and its relationship to slavery that the essay does not address." The fact that I had not discussed slavery seemed to me a peculiar basis for rejecting an article in which I examined how present-day discourses about agricultural diversification and tobacco-as-heritage serve to erase the idea of tobacco farming as a contemporary practice from public awareness. This editor had a particular narrative about tobacco in mind and was unable or unwilling to see beyond that narrative in order to consider other dimensions of the story of tobacco in the United States.

Barbara Myerhoff and Jay Ruby argue that the ethnographer "must acknowledge that his or her own behavior and persona in the field are data" (1982, 26); I contend that our behavior and encounters out of the field are relevant as well. As informal interactions of the kind I describe above began to add up, I noticed that I was continually reshaping my 'sound bite' description in an attempt to make my research topic more palatable. Eventually, I realized that I needed to pay attention to these conversations rather than try to shut them down. Informal conversations about our research might be brushed off as inconsequential and unrelated to our 'actual' data gathering and analysis. This is not the case; moreover, valuing casual responses as data makes particular sense in the discipline of folklore, a field in which the study of the vernacular and the everyday is a hallmark. While the examples I have given from casual conversations are anecdotal, they nevertheless help to illuminate what is tellable and untellable about tobacco farming and farmers in the contemporary United States.

Thus, my data came to include not only what I learned through participant observation and interviews, but also my own initial assumptions about tobacco farming, along with the assumptions that emerged in conversations about the topic of my research. Reflection on this expanded data set led me to realize that these assumptions represented those narratives about tobacco farming that are tellable in public. Such narratives serve as "terministic screens" through which tobacco is differently understood. Kenneth Burke writes,

> When I speak of "terministic screens," I have particularly in mind some photographs I once saw. They were *different* photographs of the *same* objects, the difference being that they were made with different color filters. Here something so "factual" as a photograph revealed notable distinctions in texture, and even in form, depending on which color filter was used for the documentary description of the event being recorded. (1966, 45; italics original)

Understandings of tobacco farming—and, perhaps more importantly, the tobacco farmer—take on differing, often competing, textures and symbolic meanings when filtered through different discursive screens. The tellable narratives become the screens through which tobacco farming is viewed.

Tellable Narratives

In *Other People's Stories*, Amy Shuman describes tellability this way:

> Some stories are tellable but only if the teller is willing to live with existing categories for interpreting experience. Narratives impose categories on experience, but people sometimes report that their experiences don't fit the imposed category because the category unfairly judges them or insists on motivations of deserved consequences. (2005, 7–8)

Shuman goes on to describe the relationship between tellable narratives and moral positions. She argues, "How one narrates an experience can make all the difference in determining whether an event is accepted as normal or criticized as immoral or in characterizing people as victims or willing participants" (15). Shuman is most interested in tellability and untellability in regard to stories told (or not told) by individuals about particular experiences. I contend, however, that the concept of tellability can also help us to understand the interaction between public discourses and individual narratives.

The most obvious tellable narratives about tobacco—implied in questions about whether farmers smoke and how they feel about tobacco—are intertwined: 1) tobacco causes cancer and other illnesses and 2) the industry is built on exploitation. Although tobacco has had its critics since Europeans first began to consume and then grow it, only in the decades following the 1964 Surgeon General's report "Smoking and Health" has there been reliable scientific evidence of smoking's negative impact on health.[7] Since that time, public awareness of health consequences has increased dramatically, resulting in decreased tobacco use in the United States. Smoking bans in public places have been implemented increasingly in recent years, and now the danger of 'third-hand smoke' is a topic of discussion.[8] The use of tobacco in the United States has become a stigmatized practice, and tobacco a stigmatized substance.

A second tellable narrative concerns the historical relationship between tobacco farming and the enslavement of African peoples. According to Joseph C. Robert, a mid-twentieth-century tobacco historian, tobacco "created the plantation pattern. Its labor requirements soon meant hordes of African slaves. Present-day rural and racial problems below the Mason and Dixon Line are rooted in that first Southern staple, tobacco" ([1952] 1967, 15). The role of slavery on colonial plantations is central to the emplotment of the story of tobacco in American history, even though dependency on slave labor varied by region and farm size. The historical link between tobacco and slavery is strong, perhaps second only to the link between cotton and slavery.

A third, and more complex, tellable narrative is the story of tobacco as an icon of American heritage.[9] This is the story of the past importance of tobacco production in the building of a nation, as well as tobacco production as a way of life. This narrative, particularly in Kentucky—a border state—often ignores the roles of slaves and paid laborers alike in tobacco history. An undated trade association pamphlet titled "Tobacco: Deeply Rooted in America's Heritage" begins,

> Tobacco is more deeply rooted in our history than any other commodity. Its role in America's settlement, early development and eventual independence is incalculable. Commerce in tobacco was the economic salvation of the struggling Jamestown colony. Export of the golden leaf to England was the dramatic beginning of trade in the New World. Thereafter, tobacco was a powerful magnet drawing new colonizing enterprises, attracting Europeans to the colonies and creating the basis for a mighty nation and a far-flung industry. Tobacco founded communities, extended boundaries of the original colonies, drew settlers to the "new west" of Kentucky, Tennessee, Ohio and Missouri, supported schools and churches, paid for roads . . . helped build America. (Council for Burley Tobacco n.d.; ellipses original)

The narrative of tobacco heritage was actively promoted by the tobacco industry and the state in the 1970s through the 1990s, as one means of defending an industry increasingly understood as threatened.

The heritage narrative also expresses nostalgia for the tobacco culture of the more recent past—not a specific era, but a period earlier in the life of the narrator and prior to particular technological and social changes. This narrative expresses longing for a time in which tobacco was 'the glue that held families together,' a phrase I heard repeatedly from many people over the course of my fieldwork. It tells the story of tobacco production as it was once carried out by family members working together to raise the crop throughout the year: from the springtime tasks of pulling tobacco seedlings from the plant bed and setting (or transplanting) them into the field, through months spent together in the tobacco stripping room in the late fall and winter processing the cured leaf for sale. In this past period, a golden age that changes with each generation, tobacco men were respected members of the community.[10] Reflecting on growing up on a Kentucky tobacco farm, Wendell Berry writes,

> In those days, to be recognized as a "tobacco man" was to be accorded an honor such as other cultures bestowed on the finest hunters or warriors or poets. The accolade "He's a *tobacco* man!" would be accompanied by a shake of the head to indicate that such surpassing excellence was, finally, a mystery; there was more to it than met the eye. (1991, 54; italics original)

Berry is referring to his childhood here, but for some, this might more generally describe the entire period of the mid-twentieth century into the 1980s. These were the days when tobacco was tied into "pretty hands" and sold to the rhythmic chant of the tobacco auctioneer.[11] In these remembrances of times past, tobacco was the most important, if not the only, source of cash for many farm families.[12]

This heritage narrative initially shaped many of my assumptions. I lived in Kentucky in the years leading up to the end of the federal tobacco program (the late 1990s and early 2000s).[13] During this period, the family heritage narrative was particularly prevalent both in the media and in personal conversation—because those inside and outside of farming communities assumed that the end of the tobacco program would mean the end of tobacco farming in Kentucky. My own interest in what the loss of this practice would mean to farmers is hardly surprising: our intellectual arguments to the contrary notwithstanding, folklore research often focuses on aspects of culture that are thought to be endangered or disappearing.

The first two tellable tobacco narratives in public discourse, then, focus on product use and the exploitive tobacco industry of the past and present. The third focuses on tobacco farming as *heritage*—a label that, as heritage scholars have argued, ushers cultural practices and practitioners into the past, refiguring them in an attempt to replace lost economic value. According to Barbara Kirshenblatt-Gimblett, heritage "depends on display to give dying economies and dead sites a second life as exhibitions of themselves" (1998, 7). In all of these narratives, present-day farmers are conspicuously absent.

Toward the end of my fieldwork, when I asked Jonathan Shell, a farmer who was twenty years old at the time, what he thought about my many visits to his family's farm, he told me, "Well I like it. I hope you romanticize tobacco in your dissertation and you get published. That way people will start loving it." When I asked him what he meant by *romanticize,* he replied, "Just make it intimate. To where that they can see that, you know, there's hands that touch this stuff, and that there's lives that are dependent on it." This young farmer confirmed what I had come to realize: tobacco farmers have been erased from the present through their absence in contemporary narratives about tobacco and tobacco farming. They are not visible through the screens of the tellable public narratives.

A fourth tellable narrative centers on tobacco as a crop of the past, one that has been (or is being) replaced by alternative crops. This was certainly my assumption as I began my research: I believed that all tobacco farmers were actively looking for something to replace tobacco. Based on media accounts and early conversations with people in tobacco communities, I expected that I would spend most of my time collecting narratives about farmers' experiences raising a last tobacco crop on the farm that had been in the family—and producing tobacco—for generations. This assumption did not bear out. While I certainly heard some narratives of replacement, I ended up spending the majority of my time with farmers who had no intention of ceasing tobacco production anytime soon. I may have chosen an 'endangered' tradition as my topic of research, but I found something much more complex.

The replacement narrative is prevalent in the Kentucky and national media; headline after headline in recent years has proclaimed, for example, that "[b]urley is just a memory now: Bourbon [County] farmers turn their full attention to crops for Farmers Market" (Fortune 2008). Others have bid "'Goodbye' tobacco, 'hello' cukes and corn" (Brown 2000). News agencies publish stories about tobacco barns—"stately relics of a bygone era," as one National Public Radio story described them (Adams 2009)—that are either falling down or are being converted to other uses (including apartments and garlic processing facilities). This kind of media discourse, when joined with Kentucky Department of Agriculture (KDA) efforts to re-present the state as one focused on farmers' markets, local wine, agritourism, and value-added products (from salsa to cheese), contributes to a narrative that claims tobacco is actively being replaced.[14]

This particular story was bolstered by the end of the federal tobacco program in 2004. The termination of the tobacco program is, in tobacco regions, known as 'the buyout' because tobacco manufacturers financed the buyout of production quotas over a ten-year period.[15] Many understood the buyout as a welcome end to tobacco production; some even held the misperception that "buyout" meant that farmers were selling their right to raise tobacco, although it was not a true buyout in that sense. It did mean a voluntary end to tobacco production for thousands of farmers, particularly those who were ready to retire and/or those who raised a small amount of tobacco while working a full-time job off the farm. Yet despite record-low tobacco production in Kentucky in 2005 (the year after the buyout), Kentucky farmers have continued to raise far more burley and dark tobaccos than farmers in any other state (USDA 2008). Moreover, a full 50 percent of US tobacco farms are located in Kentucky (Snell 2009). The 2007 Census of Agriculture revealed that there were 8,113 tobacco farms in Kentucky that year (USDA 2009).

Farmer Sensibility to Tellability

Listening closely to those who live and work in tobacco communities made me attentive to the fact that they are, of course, keenly aware of these public discourses. In the case of the heritage narrative, farmers have co-opted the narrative of tobacco as heritage that was promoted by the industry and the state in the last decades of the twentieth century, putting it to new uses. For instance, G.B. Shell, who raised about 110 acres of burley in 2007, asked me, "Do you know how we financed the Revolutionary War?" He knew that I knew—in part, because he'd told me before—but I asked him to tell me anyway. He continued:

> You ever been to Washington? You see what's around the Capitol, top of the Capitol, goes all the way around it. Tobacco leaves. We borrowed money from France, and they mortgaged the tobacco crop. [. . .] Whenever these people put down tobacco so bad, they're putting down the whole country.[16]

For this farmer, the importance of tobacco money in American history is not merely about the distant past. It continues to be meaningful today, just as tobacco income continues to be relevant to contemporary farmers.

Many farmers expressed their awareness of the narrative that connects tobacco and illness. In one of the first interviews I conducted, Kathleen Bond, who raised tobacco with her husband and his family until 2003, told me, "One thing that's really changed is when we got married and people raised tobacco it was a good, honest way to make a living. And at the time that we got out, if you raised tobacco, you were dirt, you know, you were contributing to the cancer." The public narrative of what it means to be a tobacco farmer has shifted dramatically, as what was once among the most respected of occupational identities in local understandings became tarnished by tying the farmer to a cancer-causing product. Kevan Evans, a former tobacco farmer who, with his daughter, now runs an agritourism operation that includes an orchard and farm stand with events that cater to families, had a similar experience. According to Evans:

> And it got to a point where, you really couldn't go out—You know if you went out of the state and they said, "What do you do?" "Well I'm a tobacco farmer," you know—I mean they kinda frowned on you. You know but I can go out and say, "Well I'm a vegetable farmer." "Oh okay, yeah! Let's talk about it."[17]

Another former tobacco farmer, Jerry Bond, told me,

> There was a time, there was a time when tobacco farmers were proud. And they were proud of their product, and they were proud of their work, and they were—a lot of little towns were built on tobacco farmers, money that tobacco made. But that pride doesn't exist any more. Tobacco farmers really have become second-class citizens.

In short, *tobacco farmer,* as viewed through the screens of the tellable narratives, is now a stigmatized category.

Stigma has been most notably considered by Erving Goffman, whose conceptualization of "spoiled identity" provides a useful, if limited, starting point for understanding stigma and stigma management in face-to-face interactions between stigmatized persons and those he calls "normals," or those "who do not depart negatively from the particular expectations at issue" ([1963] 1986, 5). Goffman considers both those who are born into a stigmatized category and those who move into a stigmatized category later in life. While he recognizes that a person may move from a non-stigmatized category into one that is stigmatized, he does not discuss the consequences of the movement from 'normal' to stigmatized of an entire category in which a person has lived her or his life, as is the case with tobacco farmers. In other words, *tobacco farmer* was once a category that was highly respected (as demonstrated, for instance, by Wendell Berry's statement, above); it is now stigmatized. Farmers over the age of about fifty have experienced this movement in their lifetimes.

Goffman also limits the possible responses of stigmatized persons; his primary concern in this discussion, after all, is "management" of stigma. In contrast, more recent studies allow a greater degree of agency for the stigmatized. For instance, Bruce G. Link and Jo C. Phelan argue that "people artfully dodge or constructively challenge stigmatizing processes" (2001, 378). They go beyond Goffman's theory, using "challenge" to suggest an active resistance in addition to the more passive act of "management."[18] In my own experience, current and former tobacco growers both manage stigma and actively respond to it.

Importantly, the stigmatization of tobacco farmers is neither consistently applied nor consistently perceived. Not all current or former producers express or acknowledge stigma; they are more are apt to acknowledge the stigma that smokers face and then relate that stigma to themselves because of the economic losses that have resulted from declining rates of smoking.[19] Tobacco farmers who still raise tobacco often continue to take pride in being called tobacco men. It is not the inclusion in the category that they resist; rather, they resist the stigmatization of the category. One way that farmers resist the changing status of both their occupation and the crop they grow is by means of defensive statements. "It's a legal crop," they protest. "I'm not telling anybody to smoke." "Tobacco pays my bills." "Tobacco is part of our heritage."

During the course of my fieldwork I found that regardless of whether tobacco continued to be raised on their farms, women talked about tobacco stigma much more frequently than did men. One notable exception was male extension service professionals, who directly addressed this topic quite often.[20] For instance, when I asked Steve Moore, a county agricultural extension agent, about public perceptions of the crop, he replied, "If you're asking, Ann, if a tobacco farmer in Kentucky, can go to a national meeting somewhere [. . .] and stand up and say 'I'm a tobacco farmer from Kentucky' and be

FIGURE 1
Bumper stickers such as this one proclaiming, "Tobacco pays my bills," are not uncommon. Pictured here, tobacco farmer Marlon Waits. Photo by author.

proud of it—*I* think there has to be a little bit of stigma, that they don't do that."

Farmers also recognize and resist the narrative of tobacco-as-gone. Clarence Gallagher, who raised twenty-two acres of tobacco in 2007, told me, "Even though they've had, you've seen all that negative in the paper and everything like this, tobacco has went up in price since the [year after the] buyout." Here, this farmer expressed his confidence in the sustainability of tobacco as a cash crop, and he also demonstrated his recognition of a media discourse that does not adequately reflect his experiences and observations.

Another county agricultural extension agent, Dan Grigson, told me that the health consequences of tobacco use make it "really hard to tell the true story of tobacco and how good it is for Kentucky and the other states that grow it." This agent argued that tobacco's continued profitability and important role in the state's economy is a story that can no longer be told. The narrative of the economic

importance of tobacco is just as 'true' as the narrative of the consequences of tobacco use, yet it has become untellable. Also untellable in
public discourses—and obscured by the screen of tellable discourses—
is what is true for tobacco farmers: they continue to raise tobacco
because they are still able to make a living raising tobacco.

The Untellable Narrative of Tobacco Farming

As my fieldwork progressed, I realized that I was approaching tobacco
production as "a way of life"—as it is often described in the heritage
narrative—and not as an occupation. But farmers taught me over and
over that they continue to produce tobacco primarily because it provides an income. Two examples from my interviews illustrate this point.

One farmer told me in the spring of 2007, "I get asked every now
and then 'Why [are] you raising, still raising tobacco?' 'Tradition' 's
what I tell 'em." Later in the interview I attempted to follow up on
what he meant by *tradition*:

> Ann Ferrell (AF): You said earlier that people, when people ask
> why you grow tobacco you say "tradition"—can
> you say more about what you mean by that?
>
> Martin Henson (MH): Oh it's just . . . sum it up in one word. [*laugh-
> ing*] Well uh, I still use it—[for] income. Uh—
>
> AF: [*overlapping*] But is it just about income?
>
> MH: But I just tell people 'tradition,' you know,
> cause uh, you know. Uh, income. And uh, I
> still uh, I've got neighbors that uh, go into
> vegetables and stuff like that.
>
> AF: Mm-hmm.
>
> MH: I still think tobacco's easier than vegetables.
> I haven't got into the vegetables, but uh, I
> don't like to pick beans. Be hard on my back.
> [*slight laugh*]

Most people would find it difficult to articulate the meaning of *tradition,* and this farmer's multiple false starts and uncharacteristic
hesitations suggest that this was difficult for him as well. But what

he did say—and what I didn't hear until I transcribed this interview—is important. I was surprised and embarrassed to hear my own resistance to him linking tradition with income when I asked, "But is it just about income?" I suppose I wanted this farmer to talk about intangible aspects of tradition—perhaps to wax on about his emotional relationship with the crop—and instead he was telling me that tobacco is important because it continues to provide income for his family, and that its economic value is central to his understanding of it as 'a tradition.'

Here, then, this farmer was not telling me that he was emotionally bound to the crop or even, in Richard Handler and Jocelyn Linnekin's terms, to his "symbolic construction" of the crop as it represents a way of life (1984, 273). These factors may be important, but tobacco is also both what he knows best and what he is materially equipped to grow, and he is bound by material and economic ties to the crop that are part of his understanding of tobacco as 'traditional' for him. For this farmer and many others, the tangible and intangible values of the crop are tied together, making 'replacement' difficult, if not impossible.

In another instance, my question suggested that a farmer might keep raising tobacco even if other opportunities would be more profitable. The following exchange took place in an interview with Roger Quarles:

> Ann Ferrell: But did it—was it important to you to continue growing some amount of tobacco, despite other opportunities that you had? Or—
>
> Roger Quarles: Well, uh . . . You gotta understand I never did particularly love growing tobacco. I did it because it was a business opportunity.[21]

Clearly, I again wanted to hear about an emotional attachment to the crop, not just an economic one, and he could sense that. While many other farmers told me that they do enjoy—even love—raising tobacco, I was told many times that no matter how much anybody might enjoy it, no one enjoyed it enough (or was stupid enough) to keep doing it if it didn't pay.

Because folklorists study cultural expressions, we are most often interested in symbolic meaning. All too often, this means that we ignore the very real economic values of the traditions we study, particularly when they are occupational. Occupational studies by folklorists have sought to "demonstrate the existence of the aesthetic impulse in the workplace" (Jones 1984, 176), as though the impulse to create art is always separate from the very real need to make a living. In the case of tobacco farming, the economic and symbolic values of tobacco have been separated discursively in the dominant narratives. As I carried out, talked about, and later wrote up my research, I needed to bring these values together again. As farmers and I discussed the importance of documenting this tradition—as I explained to them that our interviews would be archived at the Kentucky Historical Society, for instance—they wanted me to know that tobacco continues to be economically important, a fact that has become largely untellable in public discourses.[22]

From Tellability to Untellability: A Chronology

Not only was the economic importance of tobacco once tellable, it was once the dominant narrative of tobacco production. The Kentucky Department of Agriculture (KDA) spent decades arguing, in the pages of its newsletter, that tobacco was central to the Kentucky economy. Because the KDA is a state agency headed by an elected Commissioner of Agriculture, its newsletter provides a unique window into the changing political status of tobacco over the second half of the twentieth century and into the twenty-first. Between the 1940s, when the KDA newsletter began, through the first decade of the twenty-first century, the economic importance of tobacco moved from a self-evident fact, to a centerpiece in defense of the threatened industry, to an untellable narrative.

In the 1940s and into the 1950s, tobacco's economic import was unquestioned. A March 1944 article makes it clear that the KDA embraced tobacco and that increased smoking rates were understood as good for Kentucky. "Increased home consumption, plus shipments overseas to our soldiers and allied countries" were praised by the Commissioner of Agriculture, who urged farmers to maximize per acre production in order to keep up with demand (Robertson 1944).

A decade later, things were beginning to change. In the 1950s, growing medical evidence about the effects of smoking began to capture public attention. *Reader's Digest* published a series of articles on the dangers of smoking at midcentury, beginning with an article titled

"How Harmful are Cigarettes?" (Riis 1950), followed by "Cancer by the Carton" (Norr 1952) and many others. In 1954, the American Cancer Society released a report, first to the American Medical Association and then to the public, which found that the rate of death from lung cancer for heavy smokers was sixty-four times that of non-smokers (Wagner 1971, 78). None of this medical research was mentioned in the KDA newsletter. However, the tobacco narrative changed markedly in the newsletter in the mid- to late 1950s. For instance, the September 1955 issue features a full-page cover photo of a field of tobacco and a tobacco barn with the caption, "Kentucky's most

FIGURE 2
The Kentucky Department of Agriculture reminds readers
that tobacco is "Kentucky's Most Profitable Tradition."
(Kentucky Department of Agriculture Bulletin, September 1955.
Courtesy of the Kentucky Department for Libraries and Archives)

profitable tradition" (KDA 1955). The timing of an increasingly expressed self-consciousness about tobacco in the KDA newsletter suggests that rather than attempting to answer critics directly, as they later would, the KDA deployed a rhetorical defense based on tobacco as an economic mainstay.

Reports and photographs from the tobacco marketing season, when farmers received compensation for the year's work, were once featured annually in the newsletter. A December 1960 issue exemplifies this coverage, with two front-page photos of market openings highlighted by a caption reading, "Scenes such as the one above are being repeated dozens of times daily as the most important event of the year, the tobacco marketing season, occurs in Kentucky again" (KDA 1960, 1). From the 1960s through the 1980s, as tobacco became increasingly threatened by "constant attacks . . . from health organizations" (KDA 1967) and later by increased taxation and imported leaf, the rhetoric of the newsletter became increasingly defensive: the tobacco industry was understood to be in an "economic crisis." Coverage of tobacco increased and changed in tone upon the release of the Surgeon General's 1964 report "Smoking and Health" in January of that year. The front page of the February 1964 issue of the KDA newsletter included an article celebrating the centennial of the year that white burley, the strain of the plant that led to an increased use of burley in tobacco products, had been discovered on a Bracken County farm (1964a). This issue also included excerpts from the Commissioner of Agriculture's testimony to a House Tobacco Subcommittee about the need for additional tobacco research. The administrator's statement that "the tobacco business is at a crisis" began the explicit rhetoric of "tobacco in crisis" that would continue into the 1980s (KDA 1964b, 1–2).

The crisis to which the commissioner referred was, of course, the Surgeon General's report. His defense was one that I have heard countless times and in various forms from people in tobacco communities. In this mantra, everything tobacco has enabled is listed in a rhythmic chant:

> In my state, tobacco prices set real estate values; bring good times, or bad, for our economy; furnish additional money to go to Detroit for autos, trucks and tractors; permit homes to be modernized; and often times make a college education possible for deserving young men and women. (2)

Tobacco queen and princess contests were common in this period, and their role in the economic discourse became explicit in October 1970, when the KDA announced that "[t]alent [would] not be a factor" in the 1970 Burley Belle pageant. Instead, the contestants would be judged on their recitation of an essay that they were each to write on the topic "What Burley Tobacco Means to Kentucky." According to the KDA, the competition was "designed as a means of encouraging general interest in the importance of burley tobacco as the major cash crop in Kentucky" (KDA 1970, 1).

Later in the decade, the commissioner's comments summarized the familiar narrative: "Here in Kentucky, burley tobacco is, as we all know, the economic mainstay of our farmers" (Harris 1976, 2). According to the head of the Farm Bureau, in 1978 tobacco was to Kentucky "what the stock market is to Wall Street, autos to Detroit, and tourists to Florida. Take away tobacco, and you've taken away Kentucky's economic soul" (Huddleston 1978, 6). I came across a number of such comparative statements, and here "economic soul" demonstrates the interweaving of the economic and symbolic values of tobacco.

The Commissioner of Agriculture's message in November 1978 was focused on R. J. Reynolds's "Pride in Tobacco" campaign, which he used as entry into another discussion of tobacco's economic importance to Kentucky, one that paired heritage and economy: "Let's not lose sight of just how important this great crop and the people who grow, buy and process it really are to the heritage and economy of our commonwealth." He then spoke of the "individual freedom" to smoke and the "harassment" that smokers faced, concluding, "I call upon all Kentuckians who farm, sell, transport or process our crop to fight to retain tobacco as a viable product of our agriculture community. Kentucky needs tobacco and tobacco needs the support of all Kentuckians" (Harris 1978, 2).

In late 1986, Commissioner Boswell expressed his hope that 1987 would be a better year for tobacco farmers because "[t]obacco is what pays the bills" (KDA 1986, 2); several months later, the increased efforts to raise cigarette taxes beginning in the late 1980s were represented as an "attack on Kentucky's economy" (KDA 1987, 8). In the 1990s, the tone of the newsletter gradually changed once again: the commissioners no longer argued for tobacco's economic importance, and stories about tobacco became few and far between.

Tobacco critics 'loose with facts'
claims 'Pride in Tobacco' chairman

"Pride in Tobacco," an information program designed to unite the
tobacco community to support the
region's most important agricultural

**William D. Hobbs displays the logo for
the "Pride in Tobacco" campaign.
The thumbs-up sign and tobacco leaf
background are symbolic of the hope
for the tobacco industry.**

commodity, was expanded to Kentucky and six other tobacco states Nov. 1,
by the R. J. Reynolds Tobacco Company.

William D. Hobbs, chairman of
the North Carolina-based company,
told a gathering of press, state officials
and tobacco industry leaders that the
best way to preserve Kentucky's
tobacco economy is for those who
rely on tobacco to take an active
role in supporting the industry.

"Pride in Tobacco" is an information program geared to the
agribusiness community," Hobbs said.
"We hope, through this ongoing
effort, to make everyone more aware
of the importance of tobacco—to
growers, manufacturers, related in-
dustries and to the entire economic
and social fabric."

The announcement of the program was simultaneously transmitted
live to five cities in Kentucky. A
special telecommunications system
was used to link Frankfort with
Owensboro, Carrollton, Glasgow, Lexington, and Louisville.

Deputy Commissioner of Agriculture John Anderson welcomed the

program on behalf of Commissioner
Tom Harris, and urged all members
of the Kentucky agribusiness community to give their full support to
implementing the program.

Anderson emphasized that tobacco accounts for over 46% of the
cash crop receipts in Kentucky, and
that it is a significant agricultural
commodity in 118 of the state's
120 counties. He added that tobacco
is still largely a family farm operation,
and that many of these farms would
cease to exist without the tobacco
industry.

Hobbs said the "Pride in Tobacco" program was prompted by increasing anti-tobacco pressure.

"Many of our critics have been
very free with words and loose with
facts," he added.

It is expected that every tobacco
warehouse will help distribute in-
formational brochures and other
materials which Hobbs said will
outline the tobacco industry's side
of the public smoking situation,
tobacco's impact on the economy,
current smoking and health facts,
and the tax burden on tobacco.

FIGURE 3
"R.J. Reynolds' "Pride in Tobacco" campaign announced in the Kentucky
Department of Agriculture newsletter as a means of defending the tobacco
industry as concerns about health risks increased. (Kentucky Agricultural News,
November 1978. Courtesy of the Kentucky Department for Libraries and
Archives)

By the late 1990s tobacco had all but disappeared from the pages of
the KDA newsletter, replaced by "alternative" agriculture, ranging from
vegetable production to goats, vineyards, orchards, and value-added
products. Perhaps most amazingly, the 2004 tobacco buyout—widely
touted as "one of the most dramatic changes in any US agricultural
policy over the last half century" (Tiller 2005)—went almost entirely
unmentioned in the pages of the newsletter. Despite the continued
economic importance of tobacco for over 29,000 Kentucky farmers at
the time of the buyout, the narrative of tobacco as the economic mainstay of the state was no longer tellable.[23] Over lunch one day in 2007,

I asked an extension agent about the absence of tobacco on state web-sites and in state publications; he told me that it had been at least ten years since "the face of Kentucky" had been represented as based in tobacco.

According to Diane Goldstein, "Making suppositions about what is untellable, and therefore about what is absent from the tradition, may seem to some to be pushing the envelope a bit in terms of substantiating our observations. Methodologically, however, the process of locating absence is not very different from observing patterns that are *present*" (2009, 249 italics original). The chronology I have traced in the KDA newsletters reveals much about the changing status of this crop and those who grow it, precisely because the pattern of news coverage has been so markedly disrupted. Writing about "narratives of progress and preservation" in Appalachia, Mary Hufford notes that "coal camps in their postindustrial incarnation don't fit into the state's grand narrative" (2002, 112). Similarly, tobacco—as a stigmatized tradition—has lost its place in official narratives about Kentucky agriculture even as tobacco production continues there. I was able to trace the changing status of tobacco in Kentucky by analyzing the KDA newsletter—using archival evidence that could be classified as 'conventional' data.[24] However, without attention to less conventional sources of information—particularly, to casual conversations beyond 'the field'—I may not have begun to ask the questions that led me to the archive.

Conclusions

It was with both the tellable and untellable narratives in mind that I set out to communicate to my Vermont audience that "there's hands that touch this stuff, and [. . .] lives that are dependent on it." I struggled to pull them into the perspective of Kentucky burley producers so that they would be willing to hear about my research, and in doing so I called first on currently tellable narratives about tobacco production. I referenced heritage ("Imagine that you are a fifth-generation farmer"), disappearance ("of a farm product that is now in less demand," "being imported from overseas"), and health risks ("the product is associated with illness and death"). In order to prepare my audience to hear what has become untellable about tobacco farming and farmers, I relied upon their knowledge about the current Vermont dairy industry, which is often discussed using rhetoric remarkably similar to the crisis rhetoric of tobacco in earlier decades.[25] "Now imagine that product is milk. What would that mean in Vermont?" This audience responded with comments and questions that indicated that I had made the topic palatable and interesting to them. Afterwards, one participant told me that by opening with a comparison between tobacco and milk, I had made it easier for the participants to identify with—rather than judge—these farmers.

This presentation might have gone very differently had I not expanded my research to include both the tellable and untellable narratives about tobacco. I was able to uncover the tellable narratives about tobacco production only by adopting a different understanding of what constitutes data. My data came to include informal conversations that took place far outside the field, as well as my own assumptions that I carried with me into the field. As I transcribed my interviews, I listened as much to my own questions as to my interviewees' responses. Doing so led me to important realizations about the tellable narratives of tobacco production, and therefore the context in which farmers live and work. Just as importantly, my assumptions were challenged by my more conventional data, as farmers taught me that what is truest for them—the fact that tobacco continues to pay their bills—has become untellable.

While debates continue within the field of folklore about whether we should be 'advocates' or engage in 'politics,' my experience with tobacco production highlights the fact that we are already engaged in advocacy, even as we undertake something so seemingly non-political as describing our research to strangers at a baby shower. We must pay attention to data from nonconventional sources in order to hear the stories that are and are not being told. The narratives that have become untellable may turn out to tell the stories of what matters most to the participants in our research.

Notes

1. I have conducted fieldwork in the burley tobacco region of Central Kentucky since 2005. Although the major period of my research was the 2007 crop year (from January 2007 through February 2008), my research continues today. All interviews related to this project are archived in the collections of the Kentucky Oral History Commission and are used here with permission.

2. In Vermont, dairy farming is a multi-generational farming tradition. The state's dairy products account for about 75 percent of farm receipts (Vermont Dairy Promotion Council, n.d.).

3. Also see Patrick Mullen's (2002) suggestion that ethnographers should actively seek out and include "unspeakable" stories by examining narratives from multiple sources, both oral and written.

4. Under the federal tobacco program—a component of the Agricultural Adjustment Act passed in the New Deal era—tobacco farmers agreed to growing quotas in exchange for price supports. A *quota* (also referred to as an *allotment* or *base*) was the maximum amount of tobacco that could be grown on a portion of land; it was adjusted each year based on a formula that determined how much tobacco would be needed by tobacco companies and buyers. Tobacco could not be sold without proof of ownership of a quota. A *price support* was the minimum price that could be paid for a pound of tobacco of a particular type and grade; it too changed each year.

5. See Linda Dégh's (1975) work on the life history of four Hungarian immigrant farmers of tobacco in the Canadian tobacco belt. Throughout this chapter I use the phrase *tobacco communities* to refer to communities in which residents—farmer and non-farmer alike—have historically depended on tobacco income. While not everyone in such communities ever raised tobacco, many worked for tobacco farmers when they were young, sold groceries or farm implements to tobacco farmers, or were otherwise involved in the tobacco economy and culture. Therefore, people living in tobacco communities have historically been more likely to share particular knowledge of and perspectives on tobacco than those outside such communities (see Kingsolver 2012).

6. I am not alone in having had this experience. Wendell Berry writes, "Because I have written a good bit about farmers who raise tobacco and because I have often spoken in defense of the tobacco program, I often fall into conversations on the subject with people who are indignant. These conversations are always fragmentary because of the great complexity of the subject, and I have never been satisfied with any of them. And so I would like now to attempt something like a complete dialogue" (1991, 57). The remainder of this essay is a conversation with an imagined stubborn adversary. Berry describes tobacco as a "red herring" for the many evils of modern life (from gas-guzzling automobiles to reduced access to local foods) and argues that there are limited alternatives available to tobacco farmers.

7. For instance, King James I of England wrote *A Counter-Blaste to Tobacco* in 1604, in which he blasted the claims then being made that tobacco had health benefits, particularly that it was a cure-all for numerous ailments and their opposites (e.g., James questions tobacco's ability to both awaken the minds of users and to help them to sleep). James also blasted the users of tobacco and the "sinnes and vanities" committed by them when they "take" tobacco (Stuart [1604] 1954, 29), and he blasted the English for imitating not only the French and Spanish in the use of tobacco, but also (and most offensively) the Indians.

8. A 2009 *New York Times* article by Roni Caryn Rabin called attention to "third-hand smoke," or "the term being used to describe the invisible yet toxic

brew of gases and particles clinging to smokers' hair and clothing, not to mention cushions and carpeting."

9. See Sullivan 1999 for an overview of the history of the crop and its uses in the Americas.

10. See Ferrell 2013 for a discussion of the Golden Age of tobacco production, a period that is not a fixed time period, but rather a fluid period that idealizes the narrator's father or grandfather as the model of the 'tobacco man' identity.

11. Leaves of cured tobacco were long tied into what is referred to as a *hand* in preparation for sale. A hand of burley tobacco was formed as the leaves were stripped from the stem in a particular grade. The stems were held tightly in one hand, leaves pointed toward the floor. When a handful had been stripped, a leaf of the same grade, called a tie leaf, was wrapped around the stems multiple times and then woven through the stems, holding the hand together. Simple as this may sound, tying a "pretty" hand of tobacco is far from easy. It is a skill in which farmers took great pride, and one not believed to be shared equally among everyone working in a stripping room. In the early 1980s, burley farmers began packaging their tobacco into bales instead of tying it in hands. While farmers today see baling as a necessary technological change, there is a great deal of nostalgia for the tying of hands, and some believe that tobacco was of better quality prior to the move to baling (see Ferrell 2013). The tobacco auction is now nearly gone; beginning in 2000, many farmers began growing tobacco on contract with particular companies, a practice that was solidified with the end of the tobacco program in 2004.

12. For instance, according to the Census of Agriculture, tobacco was grown on 80 percent of Kentucky farms in 1959 compared to 10 percent in 2007. Statements about how "it used to be that tobacco could pay for a farm" are often repeated. Farmers often told me that when the tobacco program was in place, the tobacco quota tied to a farm served as collateral for a farm mortgage and that the sale of one's tobacco at the end of the year provided the cash needed for the annual mortgage payment (as well as the grocery bill, Christmas presents, etc.). Obviously, this did not change suddenly with the end of the program; rather, as farm expenses rose much faster than tobacco prices over the decades, additional income (whether from other farm products or off-farm work) became increasingly necessary.

13. Discussions of ending the tobacco program go back decades, but they became serious beginning in the 1980s; by the late 1990s the end of the program was understood by all involved to be inevitable.

14. See Ferrell 2012 and Ferrell 2014 for a discussion of the gendered challenges of diversifying away from tobacco.

15. See Stull 2009 and Ferrell 2013 for overviews of the end of the federal tobacco program.

16. Tobacco adorns the columns in the Small Senate Rotunda, reconstructed in 1816 after the 1814 fire, as well as the twenty-eight columns lining the Hall of Columns, constructed in the mid-nineteenth century. Other agricultural representations in the Capitol include corncob capitals (Architect of the Capitol, n.d.).

17. In all interview transcriptions, an em-dash (—) is used to denote that the speaker has stopped suddenly and redirected him or herself.

18. By *passive* I mean that "management" involves a certain level of acceptance of stigma rather than the active resistance implicit in Link and Phelan's "challenge." I do not mean that Goffman does not describe 'active' management strategies; such strategies are one of his major concerns.

19. Ironically, this relates back to my argument regarding the inseparability of the product and the producer.

20. By *extension professionals* I refer to employees of the University of Kentucky Cooperative Extension Service who work at the university or in county offices.

21. Although Roger Quarles was the president of the Burley Tobacco Growers Cooperative Association at the time of our interview, he spoke to me as a tobacco farmer and not a representative of the Co-op.

22. I often stressed to farmers that their interviews were not only important to me, but that they were to be archived at the Kentucky Historical Society (in the collections of the Kentucky Oral History Commission) so that future generations could also learn from them. This was an attempt on my part to express my strong belief in the historical importance of their individual voices and their place in the historical record. It was also an effort to build ethos not only as a student from an out-of-state university who was interested in their stories, but also as a researcher with ties to a respected state institution. I wanted each of the farmers to know that their story was important to me and to others. Debora Kodish has described (and challenged) the narrative formula of 'discovery' that folklorists have often relied upon in describing first encounters with (perhaps only seemingly) reluctant tradition bearers "awakened to the new worth of their heritage, transformed by the folklorist's visit" (1993, 574). My attempts at assuring tobacco farmers may have also reproduced the very public discourses of tobacco as heritage and history that I identify and critique here. As a result, some of my interviewees made sure to let me know that tobacco is not just history.

23. According to census figures, tobacco was grown on 29,237 Kentucky farms in 2002 (USDA 2009).

24. For a fuller analysis of the Kentucky Department of Agriculture newsletters from the 1940s through 2007, see Ferrell 2013.

25. The economic crisis faced by dairy farmers is a central element of current public discourse about Vermont agriculture. Milk producers were being paid half of what it cost them to produce milk at the time that I spoke to this group in 2009, and the congressional delegations from dairy-dependent states such as Vermont called for emergency aid payments followed by long-term solutions in order to balance supply and demand—this was precisely the purpose of the now-defunct federal tobacco program. For instance, Vermont Senator Bernie Sanders was quoted as having said at a "dairy town hall meeting" that "[t]he bottom line [is that] the preservation [of] family-based dairy is of enormous consequence, not only to farmers but to [the] economy of the state of Vermont and to our entire way of life" (Flagg 2010, 18A).

References

Adams, Noah. 2009. "Tobacco Barns: Stately Relics of a Bygone Era." *National Public Radio Morning Edition*, November 28. http://www.npr.org/templates/story/story.php?storyId=6536351.

Architect of the Capitol. n.d. "Architectural Features." http://www.aoc.gov/cc/architecture/index.cfm. Accessed 15 September 2008.

Berry, Wendell. 1991. "The Problem of Tobacco." In *Sex, Economy, Freedom, & Community: Eight Essays*, 53–68. New York: Pantheon.

Bond, Jerry and Kathleen. 2005. Interview by author. Digital recording. August 31. Kentucky Oral History Commission, Kentucky Historical Society, Frankfort, Kentucky.

Bond, Jerry. 2005. Interview by author. Digital recording. September 15. Kentucky Oral History Commission, Kentucky Historical Society, Frankfort, Kentucky.

Boswell, David E. 1986. "Commissioner's Message." *Kentucky Agricultural News*, October, 2.

Brown, Justin. 2000. "'Goodbye' Tobacco, 'Hello' Cukes and Corn." *Christian Science Monitor* 92 (190): 3.

Burke, Kenneth. 1966. "Terministic Screens." In *Language as Symbolic Action: Essays on Life, Literature, and Method*, 44–62. Berkeley and Los Angeles: University of California Press.

Capehart, Tom. 2007. "US Tobacco Import Update 2005/06." Electronic Outlook Report from the Economic Research Service, United States Department of Agriculture, May. www.ers.usda.gov.

Council for Burley Tobacco. n.d. "Tobacco: Deeply Rooted in America's Heritage." Pamphlet.

Dégh, Linda. 1975. *People in the Tobacco Belt: Four Lives*. Ottawa: National Museums of Canada.

Evans, Kevan and Jenny. 2006. Interview by Kara Keeton. Digital recording. September 26. Kentucky Oral History Commission, Kentucky Historical Society, Frankfort, Kentucky.

Ferrell, Ann K. 2012. "Doing Masculinity: Gendered Challenges to Replacing Burley Tobacco in Central Kentucky." *Agriculture and Human Values* 29 (2): 137–49.

———. 2013. *Burley: Kentucky Tobacco in a New Century*. Lexington: University Press of Kentucky.

———. 2014. "Cutting a Thousand Sticks of Tobacco Makes a Boy a Man: Traditionalized Performances of Masculinity in Occupational Contexts." In *Unsettling Assumptions: Tradition, Gender, Drag*, eds. Pauline Greenhill and Diane Tye, 38–55. Logan: Utah State University Press.

Flagg, Kathryn. 2010. "Ag Chief: Consensus Needed for Dairy Reform." *Addison County Independent*, February 18, 1, 18A.

Fortune, Beverly. 2008. "Burley Is Just a Memory Now." *Lexington Herald-Leader*, July 6.

Gallagher, Clarence. 2007. Interview by author. Digital recording. June 20. Kentucky Oral History Commission, Kentucky Historical Society, Frankfort, Kentucky.

Goffman, Erving. (1963) 1986. *Stigma: Notes on the Management of Spoiled Identity.* New York: Simon and Schuster.

Goldstein, Diane G. 2009. "The Sounds of Silence: Foreknowledge, Miracles, Suppressed Narratives, and Terrorism: What Not Telling Might Tell Us." *Western Folklore* 68:235–55.

Handler, Richard, and Jocelyn Linnekin. 1984. "Tradition, Genuine or Spurious." *Journal of American Folklore* 97:273–90.

Harris, Thomas O. 1976. "Commissioner's Message." *Kentucky Agricultural News,* January, 2.

———. 1978. "Commissioner's Message." *Kentucky Agricultural News,* November, 2.

Henson, Martin. 2007. Interview by author. Digital recording. April 27. Kentucky Oral History Commission, Kentucky Historical Society, Frankfort, Kentucky.

Huddleston, Gary. 1978. "Anita Bryant to Head Entertainment at State Farm Bureau Meeting." *Kentucky Agricultural News* 9 (5): 6.

Hufford, Mary. 2002. "Reclaiming the Commons: Narratives of Progress, Preservation, and Ginseng." In *Culture, Environment, and Conservation in the Appalachian South,* edited by Benita J. Howell, 100–20. Champaign: University of Illinois Press.

Jones, Michael Owen. 1984. "Introduction." *Western Folklore* 43:172–78.

Kentucky Department of Agriculture (KDA). 1955. "Kentucky's Most Profitable Tradition." *Kentucky Department of Agriculture Bulletin* 11 (8): 1.

———. 1960. [Photographs with captions.] *Kentucky Department of Agriculture Bulletin* 15 (12): 1.

———. 1964a. "Centennial Year of Burley Tobacco." *Kentucky Department of Agriculture Bulletin* 19 (2): 1–2.

———. 1964b. "Butler Testifies to Need for Tobacco Studies." *Kentucky Department of Agriculture Bulletin* 19 (2): 1–2.

———. 1967. "Tobacco and Health Chief Topic at Meeting of Burley & Dark Dealers." *Kentucky Department of Agriculture Bulletin* 22 (10): 1–2.

———. 1970. "Kentucky Burley Festival Announces Plans for 'Burley Belle' Scholarship Pageant." *Kentucky Agricultural News* 2 (5): 1.

———. 1986. "1986 Was Year of Ups and Downs, but 1987 Should Promise More." *Kentucky Agricultural News* 17 (4): 2.

———. 1987. "Proposed Cigarette Tax Would Cost Many Jobs." *Kentucky Agricultural News* 18 (2): 8.

Kingsolver, Ann E. 2012. *Tobacco Town Futures: Global Encounters in Rural Kentucky.* Long Grove, IL: Waveland Press.

Kirshenblatt-Gimblett, Barbara. 1998. *Destination Culture: Tourism, Museums, and Heritage.* Berkeley and Los Angeles: University of California Press.

Kodish, Debora. 1993. "Absent Gender, Silent Encounter." In *Feminist Theory and the Study of Folklore,* edited by Susan Tower Hollis, Linda Pershing, and M. Jane Young, 41–50. Champaign: University of Illinois Press.

Labov, William, and Joshua Waletzky. 1967. "Narrative Analysis: Oral Versions of Personal Experience." In *Essays on the Verbal and Visual Arts,* edited by June L. Helm, 12–44. Seattle: University of Washington Press.

Link, Bruce G., and Jo C. Phelan. 2001. "Conceptualizing Stigma." *Annual Review of Sociology* 27:363–85.

Moore, Steve. 2007. Interview by author. Digital recording. November 30. Kentucky Oral History Commission, Kentucky Historical Society, Frankfort, Kentucky.

Mullen, Patrick B. 2002. Review of *Swinging in Place: Porch Life in Southern Culture*, by Jocelyn Hazelwood Donlon. *American Quarterly* 54 (3): 507–13.

Myerhoff, Barbara, and Jay Ruby. 1982. "Introduction." In *A Crack in the Mirror: Reflexive Perspective in Anthropology*, edited by Jay Ruby, 1–35. Philadelphia: University of Pennsylvania Press.

Norr, Roy. 1952. "Cancer by the Carton." *Reader's Digest*, December, 738–39.

Quarles, Roger. 2008. Interview by author. Digital recording. January 31. Kentucky Oral History Commission, Kentucky Historical Society, Frankfort, Kentucky.

Rabin, Roni Caryn. 2009. "A New Cigarette Hazard: 'Third-Hand Smoke.'" *New York Times*, January 2. http://www.nytimes.com/2009/01/03/health/research/03 smoke.html.

Riis, Roger William. 1950. "How Harmful Are Cigarettes?" *Reader's Digest*, January, 1–11.

Robert, Joseph C. (1952) 1967. *The Story of Tobacco in America*. Chapel Hill: University of North Carolina Press.

Robertson, Elliot. 1944. "Commissioner's Column." *Kentucky Marketing Bulletin* 1 (2): 1.

Sacks, Harvey. 1995. Harvey Sacks: *Lectures on Conversation: Volumes I & II*. Ed., Gail Jefferson. Oxford: Blackwell.

Shell, GB and Jonathan. 2008. Interview by author. Digital recording. January 22. Kentucky Oral History Commission, Kentucky Historical Society, Frankfort, Kentucky.

Shuman, Amy. 2005. *Other People's Stories: Entitlement Claims and the Critique of Empathy*. Champaign: University of Illinois Press.

Snell, Will. 2009. "Census Data Reveal Significant and a Few Surprising Changes in Kentucky's Tobacco Industry." Department of Agricultural Economics, University of Kentucky College of Agriculture, February. http://www.ca.uky. edu/agecon/Index.php?p=259.

Stuart, James. (1604) 1954. *A Counter-Blaste to Tobacco*. London: Rodale Press.

Stull, Donald. 2009. "Tobacco is going, going . . . But where?" *Culture & Agriculture* 32 (2): 54–72.

Sullivan, C. W., III. 1999. "Tobacco." In *Rooted in America: Foodlore of Popular Fruits and Vegetables*, edited by David Scofield Wilson and Angus K. Gillespie, 166–87. Knoxville: University of Tennessee Press.

Tiller, Kelly. 2005. "Tobacco Buyout Top Ten." Prepared for the University of Kentucky, North Carolina State University, and the University of Tennessee, February 21. http://agpolicy.org/tobaccobuyout/tobuy/TopTen.pdf. Accessed 1 October 2005.

United States Department of Agriculture (USDA). 2008. *Kentucky Agricultural Statistics and Annual Report 2007–2008*. Washington, D.C.: National Agriculture Statistics Service.

———. 2009. "2007 Census of Agriculture: Kentucky State and County Data." National Agriculture Statistics Service. http://www.agcensus.usda.gov/Publications/ 2007/Full_Report/Volume_1, _Chapter_1_ State_Level/Kentucky/index.asp.

Vermont Dairy Promotion Council. n.d. "Vermont Dairy Facts." http://www.ver
    montdairy.com/dairy_industry/facts.
Wagner, Susan. 1971. *Cigarette Country: Tobacco in American History and Politics.*
    New York: Praeger.

ANN K. FERRELL is Associate Professor of Folk Studies, Department
of Folk Studies and Anthropology, Western Kentucky University. Her
publications include *Burley: Kentucky Tobacco in a New Century* (University
Press of Kentucky, 2013).

2 Contextualization, Reflexivity, and the Study of Diabetes-Related Stigma

MY EXAMINATION OF diabetes-related stigma serves as a reminder that the research projects we set out to do often transform during the course of fieldwork. In November 2007 I started attending a range of diabetes education and community programs in Columbus, Ohio, in order to meet people I could interview for my dissertation. My initial plan was to collect personal narratives about the dietary changes people diagnosed with diabetes were called upon to make; I hoped to analyze how their narrative framings of their foodways interacted with their narrative framings of themselves.[1] I also intended to use these narratives to examine the interactions between institutional and vernacular discourses in social life—more specifically, I was interested in how people made sense of different ways of knowing about food (e.g., nutritional, sensory, cultural) in narrative presentations of self.[2] The more I participated in these public events and programs, though, the more the events themselves became the focus of my 'researcher's gaze,' and my research interests shifted from narrative constructions of self to the ways people engaged with diabetes as a *community* issue in these venues. This shift led me to turn critical attention to processes of stigmatization (and de-stigmatization) in relation to diabetes. To examine these processes, I began a performance-based analysis of vernacular responses to diabetes-related stigma, one that sought to explore the dynamic relationships between situated speech events and larger structures of power.

A key characteristic of performance is "a higher than usual degree of reflexivity" (Kapchan 1995, 479). Of course, as Harris M. Berger and Giovanna P. Del Negro remind us, there is a "confusingly wide range of ways in which the term [reflexivity] is used" in the study of performance. Some scholars who invoke reflexivity point to language that refers to itself, while others are concerned with subjects' awareness of themselves *as* subjects, or they focus on how participants in performance events draw upon shared cultural knowledge to comment on the culture itself (2002, 63).[3] In taking a performance approach to vernacular responses to stigma that I encountered during my fieldwork, my own attention to the reflexive nature of these performances brought my focus to the practices of *contextualization* I found within them.

Noting the shift first from text to context and then from context to contextualization following the performance turn in folklore and other disciplines, Richard Bauman and Charles Briggs identify contextualization as "an active process of negotiation in which participants reflexively examine the discourse as it is emerging, embedding assessments of its structure and significance in the speech itself" (Bauman and Briggs 1990, 69). Context, then, is not merely a residual thing that somehow exists separately from a performance text, but something created in the performance encounter. Drawing on Bateson's notion of meta-communication (1972), Goffman's examination of framing (1974), and Gumperz's work on contextual cues (1982, 1992), Goodwin and Duranti similarly call attention to "the dynamic mutability of context" given "the ability of participants to rapidly invoke within the talk of the moment alternate contextual frames" (1992, 5).

Attending to the reflexive nature of the performances I experienced during my fieldwork, in this chapter I show how practices of contextualization not only generated frameworks of interpretation for communicative interactions but also served as discursive tools in vernacular efforts of de-stigmatization. Additionally, I draw upon my fieldwork experiences to enter into a broader critical conversation about the contextualizing practices often employed by researchers working with stigmatized communities. More specifically, I call attention to the ways such contextualizing practices can divide scholarly and vernacular interpretations into hierarchically ordered categories of analysis, thereby contributing to the very processes of stigmatization these researchers are seeking to disrupt.

"A type 1 diabetic is just walking down the street . . ."

Diabetes refers to a metabolic condition in which the body does not regulate blood glucose levels effectively, though the condition can take more than one form. Type 1 diabetes occurs when an autoimmune response leaves the body unable to produce insulin, a hormone necessary for regulating blood glucose levels; genetic predisposition constitutes the number one risk factor for this form of the disease. Type 2 diabetes occurs when the body does not produce enough insulin or when the body creates insulin but is unable to utilize it effectively. While there are multiple risk factors for this form of the disease—including genetic predisposition and age—type 2 diabetes is most often associated with obesity and inactive lifestyles.[4]

Type 2 diabetes offers a particularly rich site to explore the connections between bodily practices and stigma: its linkage with 'poor lifestyle choices'—particularly 'bad' eating and exercise habits, and a lack of control—can work to discredit individuals for their supposed lack of self-care (Broom and Whittaker 2004). To begin thinking about how this connection manifests in everyday interactions, consider the following example. One evening in April 2006 I attended a party at the house of a fellow graduate student in Columbus. At one point during the party, I started talking to a young, white surgeon who worked at a local hospital. When he asked me about my research interests, I offered a very brief answer to his question by saying that I wanted to explore how people make sense of their experiences with diabetes, particularly when they are diagnosed late in life and expected to make dietary changes. He asked me how I got interested in the topic, and I explained that I myself had type 1 diabetes. I also told him that I was struck by the personal narratives I had heard during "story circles" in January 2006, when performance artist Robbie McCauley visited Columbus and invited people with diabetes (primarily, though not exclusively, type 2) to share their experiences in a group setting. The surgeon began to talk about the diabetic patients he encountered in his own work, describing, for example, how some of them were so obese that several hospital staff members were required to move them. He explained, "I tend to have more sympathy for the type 1 diabetics I get than the type 2." When I asked what he meant, he explained, "A type 1 diabetic is just walking down the street and gets shot. A type 2 diabetic is in a gang, robs a liquor store, pulls a gun, and then gets shot."

This conversation was my initial entry point into thinking specifically about diabetes and stigma: the surgeon's reference to criminality provided a vivid example of the way diabetes discourse can link class, race, morality, and blame, situating type 2 diabetes and its complications as expected results of a series of bad choices. Looking more closely at references to type 2 diabetes in other communicative contexts, I quickly found that the ideas expressed by the surgeon did not exist in isolation. For instance, a saying attributed to Dr. Frank Vinicor of the Centers for Disease Control and Prevention (CDC)— one often quoted in health promotional materials and media stories about the disease—is "Genetics may load the cannon, but human behavior pulls the trigger." Such language shows us explicitly how discursive associations have formed between type 2 diabetes and what Erving Goffman calls "blemishes of individual character" (1963, 4).

Significantly, the language of blame is also used by those without 'expert' status. Consider the following comments posted online in response to Tara Parker-Pope's 2009 *New York Times* piece, "The Voices of Type 2 Diabetes," which included videos of six people with type 2 diabetes talking about their personal experiences. Commenters remarked,

> "My grand daughter has diabetes type 1. At 13 she has to control her eating, exercise and constant monitoring. And at 13 she has fantastic control. All these people in pictures are over wwight [*sic*]. Where is your control? Don't cry sympathy from me."
>
> "More than 90% of type 2 diabetes cases can be prevented through proper diet and exercise. Got pity?"
>
> "How about a discussion of TYPE 1 diabetes, by people whose disease wasn't brought on by their lifestyles or anything they did. . ."[5]

In these comments, lifestyle—or lack of control—is used to call attention squarely to individual choice as the source of blame. In her exploration of the development of knowledge and practices in health education and health promotion, Deborah Lupton explains that "[a]ll medical conditions are subject to moral judgments, based on such concepts as personal responsibility for illness and the patient's compliance with medical advice" (1995, 71). Scholars such as Robert Crawford (1977, 1980) have also examined how the growing rhetoric of 'lifestyle' and the personal responsibilities for 'at risk' behaviors gained political salience in the 1970s and '80s, leading to the stigmatization of people with so-called lifestyle diseases. As unhealthy living became causally linked to these diseases, daily practices (such as eating habits) came under the realm of medical authority though a process of what sociologist Natalie Boero terms "the professionalization of common sense" (2007, 52). In this schema, the basic tenets of healthy

living are simple, but individuals need guidance from health professionals to bring them back on track;[6] thus, healthy living becomes an issue of
compliance. As Martha Balshem points out, however, "[L]ifestyle theories of disease tend to draw from constructions of sick or high-risk
people as foolish, morally flawed, or ignorant" (1993, 24). That is, the
disease comes to be understood as a physical manifestation of problematic character traits.

When I shared the surgeon's words with an African American
community health educator I interviewed three years later, she immediately responded, "It always seems to go back to race." While the surgeon
did not identify particular racialized bodies in his comparison, this
health educator recognized in his statement a built-in stereotyping of
criminality as *always already* black.[7] Aside from the common representation of African American gangs in popular culture and mass media, the
racialization implicit in the surgeon's words is also bolstered by the
disproportionate rates of diabetes-related morbidity and mortality
among African Americans. According to the 2011 National Diabetes
Fact Sheet, diabetes is the seventh leading cause of death in the
United States, and the risk of being diagnosed with diabetes is 77%
higher among non-Hispanic blacks compared to non-Hispanic whites.
Ohio has been significantly affected by this growing epidemic among
African Americans: according to the 2010 Ohio Diabetes Fact Sheet
released by the Ohio Department of Health, the 2008 mortality rate of
blacks was more than 84% higher than that of whites; earlier, in 2004, a
Columbus Health Department survey had also shown that residents of
the Near East Side, a predominantly low-income African American
cluster of neighborhoods, were disproportionately affected by diabetes
and its complications in comparison to other parts of the city.

In *Stigma: Notes on the Management of Spoiled Identity*, Erving Goffman
begins his discussion with the body: he presents the ancient Greeks'
definition of stigma as "bodily signs designed to expose something
unusual and bad about the moral status of the signifier" (1963, 1).
Today, he argues, *stigma* refers more to a spoiled identity than to its
corporeal evidence. While this historical change has shifted the basis
of stigma toward discrediting attributes, Ann Ferrell reminds us that
the physical body still remains a central site where stigma is perceived
and experienced (2009, 211). There are two ways to spoil an identity:
one is to disclose bodily stigmata, and the other is to disclose discreditable information about the embodied individual. Type 2 diabetes

becomes a site where both types of disclosures converge. In my casual conversation with the surgeon, we can see multiple engagements with the marked body, all of which get tied to stigmatizing attributes. We see the surgeon's presentation of his patients' bodies—often obese and suffering from complications related to diabetes—as experiencing the material effects of the blemishes of individual character so often associated with diabetes, including a lack of self-control. Additionally, through the reference to criminality, we see how blemishes of individual character become associated with specifically black bodies as well, highlighting how stigma is, in the words of Goffman, "really a special kind of relationship between attribute and stereotype" (1963, 4)—a relationship in which, at least in the case of diabetes, the body is always at the forefront. Though initially the disease may be visually imperceptible, its disclosure retroactively legitimates the perceived character flaws of the individual.[8]

Goffman identifies three types of discrediting attributes: "abominations of the body," "blemishes of individual character," and "the tribal stigma of race, nation, and religion" (1963, 4).[9] While Goffman introduces these types of stigma as distinct from one another, historian Keith Wailoo describes how all three have converged within African Americans' experiences of disease in the twentieth century, "designating hidden invisible taints. . . and thereby reinforcing broader prejudices and policies" that contribute to health disparities in the United States (Wailoo 2006, 533). I would argue that the surgeon's reference to criminality also reveals a convergence of these three types of stigma, offering further support for Veena Das's claim that discursive formations of disease very often get "hooked into discursive formations of race and racism" (2001).[10]

In their article "Conceptualizing Stigma," Bruce G. Link and Jo C. Phelan argue that the term *stigma* applies when "elements of labeling, stereotyping, separation, status loss, and discrimination co-occur in a power situation" (2001, 367). Indeed, in cases like diabetes, systematic devaluing of individuals associated with certain labels can have very real health implications (Saylor 1990). At the structural level, for example, devaluation can restrict people's access to health resources, while at the individual level it can prevent people from seeking out the care they need (Link and Phelan 2001, 2006; Wailoo 2006).

If, following Link and Phelan, we understand stigma as the outcome of a process, then it is worthwhile to draw a distinction between stigma (the effect) and stigmatizing storylines (the naturalized connection between label and stereotype that lays the foundation for the effect). I use the term *storylines* deliberately here: negative attributes associated with diabetes become connected to certain emplotments that are, in turn, projected onto the life stories of the stigmatized. For example, the surgeon imagined the life story of a type 2 patient as one typified by a series of harmful choices undeserving of sympathy, an idea he communicated to me by comparing such a patient to a gang member who tries to rob a liquor store. Stigmatizing storylines occur when stereotypical categories overdetermine individual identities. Dangers arise when the power differentials structuring the relationship between negative attribute and stereotype remain unquestioned.

Early Methodological Considerations

Reflecting upon my experience with the surgeon, it became clear to me that his choice of words was as much a commentary on the immediate discursive context as it was a synthesizing evaluation of his past work experiences. I doubt, for example, that the surgeon would have offered this comparison had I not told him that I had type 1 diabetes. As he told me about his experiences with type 2 patients, his comparison demonstrated that he differentiated my condition from theirs—and me from them. It is also doubtful, I believe, that he would have used such racialized imagery if I had been a person of color. With his choice of words, he situated me, his listener, in terms of stigmatizing binaries: innocent victim versus someone undeserving of sympathy.

This experience led me to consider the following questions as I conducted my fieldwork, particularly as I came into contact with African Americans who had diabetes: To what extent do people with diabetes discursively engage with diabetes-related stigma as they talk about their experiences with the disease? And how would my embodied presence influence others' discursive engagements? Following Aaron Turner's (2000) call for reflexive practices that take into account the researcher's *physical* presence in the field, I approached this second question as a methodological one, a move toward reflexively engaging with my own fieldwork and the data I collected during that process. Seeking to approach my field research as a project of "dialogue, performance and production" (Pool 1994, 239) in a range of settings, including one-on-one interviews, informal conversations, story circles, and more formal diabetes education classes and programs, I knew I was undeniably an active participant in these settings, never a mere observer, even when I sat silently.[11]

As I began conducting interviews and observing formal and informal diabetes health education events, I made a special point in my field notes to reflect on how my body occupied the space of my fieldwork encounters. For example, when I observed adult diabetes nutrition education classes, I noted where I sat in relation to the students in the class—sometimes at the large table where the students sat, and sometimes at a smaller table set up separately for observers—so that I could reflect upon how my body's positioning in that space influenced the informal conversations I had with the students during the break. I made a point to record the ways in which people would comment on the insulin pump hooked onto my waistband, and I would reflect on whether I thought that recognition was seen as a marker of identification (e.g., "I didn't realize you had diabetes, too!") or differentiation (e.g., "I've heard good things about the pump, but my insurance doesn't cover it"). Looking back at these field notes, it has become clear to me that my interest in my embodied presence was contained within what I deemed the realm of *context*; that is, I was documenting what I recognized as the significant details of my embodied presence in order to inform what I saw to be a more 'primary,' language-focused research question that I brought to these same encounters: How do people with diabetes respond reflexively to the stigma they encounter, and what discursive resources (such as genres, claims to authority, and strategies of resignification) do they draw upon in their responses?

This research question emerged partly in response to Link and Phelan's reminder that an understanding of stigma should extend beyond how passive victims manage spoiled identities, incorporating as well how "people artfully dodge or constructively challenge stigmatizing processes" (2001, 387), a point since echoed by others (Campbell and Deacon 2006; Howarth 2006). Through a performance-based approach, I hoped to identify some of the strategies of resistance employed by people with diabetes in their conversations with me and, in the case of African American community activists and health educators, with fellow community members who either had or were at risk for diabetes.

In these settings, I expected to find critical engagements with the stigmatizing storylines of race and a lack of self-control, and I also expected that I would need to situate myself reflexively as a participant in these contexts. As my field research progressed, though, I found that my body was not contained in a clearly bounded realm of context and, moreover, that the reflexivity in others' performances and in my own methodological approach interacted in ways I did not anticipate. More specifically, I found myself encountering characterizations of my embodied self in the language of others' performative responses to stigma.

In the following sections, I offer examples of two such encounters during my field research, one that took place during a story circle led by performance artist Robbie McCauley and another that occurred during a one-on-one interview with a community member actively involved in fighting health disparities among African Americans. In both cases, I was the only non-African American in the room. In addition, although the settings and purposes were different in each case, both encounters included self-conscious responses to processes of stigmatization affecting African Americans with diabetes. In both cases, the speakers challenged these processes by reorienting the conversation away from individual attributes and toward larger systemic structures of inequality. At the same time, their incorporation of *me* into their performed challenges of stigma has led me to rethink some of the assumptions underlying my research—particularly in terms of methodological reflexivity, which I will discuss more fully in the final section.

"You didn't know that, huh?"

On November 30, 2007, after a brief period of socializing and snacking on fresh fruits, vegetables, cheese, and crackers, eleven people were sitting in chairs arranged in a circle in the main room of the small Near Eastside Healthy Lifestyle Center (NEHLC), a community center that provided its Columbus neighborhood with health programming related to the prevention, diagnosis, and treatment of diabetes.[12] Everyone had gathered to be part of a story circle facilitated by Robbie McCauley, a Boston-based African American performance artist who was conducting these circles with people whose lives have been affected in some way by diabetes.[13] In these story circles she created spaces where people could share and discuss their experiences with diabetes. In the process, McCauley facilitated conversations that engaged themes she was also exploring in *Sugar,* a solo work-in-progress that examines the interplay between her own personal experiences with diabetes and the experiences of African Americans more broadly (McCauley 2009). She had traveled to Columbus to perform *Sugar* at the Global Diabetes Summit in Columbus the following day.[14]

McCauley had been to Columbus once before, in January 2006, when she was an artist-in-residence in the Departments of Theater and Geography at The Ohio State University. I was asked to assist with McCauley's 2006 visit by Marie Cieri, an Assistant Professor in the Department of Geography, who had previously worked with her as a producer. One of my duties was to participate in two of McCauley's story circles. The first, which took place at the Multicultural Center on Ohio State's main campus, was made up mostly of individuals who had some connection to the university, including staff, students, and faculty. The second took place at the Central Community House, a community center in Columbus; Cieri and I were the only non-African Americans to participate. In both circles, most people had type 2 diabetes. Diagnosed with type 1 diabetes at the age of 13, I had always viewed diabetes as an individual problem— specifically *my* individual problem—so I was immediately struck during the second circle by the ways individual experiences were incorporated into larger community narratives of illness.

When McCauley returned to Columbus in 2007, I volunteered to help with her visit, now ready to observe her work with the eye of a researcher. On November 30, 2007, I picked her up from her hotel and drove her to the NEHLC. The evening's other participants included community residents who had diabetes or who had family members with diabetes, three staff members of the NEHLC who were also community residents, and one physician. I was the only non-African American participant.

Once everyone was seated, McCauley introduced the basic principles guiding story circles. She explained that in the circle, all participants would have a chance to speak about their experiences, and the only rule was that everybody would listen respectfully when somebody was talking. She also explained that the story circles she facilitates usually start on a theme. The last time she was in Columbus, she had asked participants to talk about their dramatic experiences with diabetes, or "diabetes as drama." While people were free to talk about any topic in the 2007 circle, McCauley was especially interested in having people share how they had found out they had the disease.

At one point during the story circle, one woman began talking about her husband's difficulty taking care of his diabetes without health insurance, and she shared a story about how they had to consider the possibility of skipping his medications because they could not afford them. After the woman finished telling her story, McCauley looked at me and said:

> Well, [*turning to me*] Sheila, [*looking around the circle*] would, when we did this before, I have to bring this up, [*laughs*] Sheila was helping the person responsible, and Sheila also has diabetes, and we were in a circle similar to this and sh- she said it couldn't, it hadn't occurred to her how hard it was for people in the circle, mainly who were African American, how hard it was to get diagnostic, diagnosis and care and so forth, and of course that brings up the whole subject of what we are looking at, at the caucus of disparities and diabetes, [*referring to the community health event taking place the following day*] but it was like, [*laughs, looking back at me*] you didn't know that, huh?

Beginning with the phrase "speaking of disparities," another woman then shared a story about a phone conversation she had with her son, who had been diagnosed with diabetes several years before. When she asked him what his hemoglobin A1c was, he did not know what she was talking about.[15] It was at this point that she learned that his doctor had never talked to him about his hemoglobin A1c levels, despite this indicator's importance in effectively monitoring blood glucose over a long period of time. McCauley replied, "It's those kinds of subtle things in diabetes that makes all the difference, because that's what it is. You don't feel like you're sick until it's too late." Her narrative is just one of many in this circle that developed the theme of health disparities experienced as a result of being stigmatized as African Americans.[16]

The story McCauley shared about my ignorance references four different contexts, all of which are important for understanding what took place during the exchange: 1) the story circle at the Central Community House in January 2006, referenced by McCauley in 2) the November 2007 story circle at the NEHLC, during a conversation about 3) health disparities faced by African Americans as a community, which is a topic that was to be addressed at 4) the community health event taking place the following day. Let me briefly sketch how each of these contexts—and its implications for meaning—becomes visible in the shape and content of her speech.

After a slight hesitation at the beginning of the stretch of discourse, McCauley addresses me directly by name ("Sheila"), before she starts to invoke the context of the earlier story circle ("when we did this before"). She then breaks frame, addressing me once again in the present: "I have to bring this up." Her quiet laughter accompanying this last phrase indicates a kind of awkwardness, an awareness of a social divide. It also sets up the story that follows as one that is at least somewhat humorous. The story returns to the frame of the earlier story circle as McCauley situates my role as a participant in that event. I am described as having two roles: the first is 'official' ("Sheila was helping the person responsible"), and the second is more personal ("and Sheila also has diabetes"). Next, McCauley explicitly draws a connection between the reported and the reporting context ("and we were in a circle similar to this"), which she reinforces later on when she describes the other participants as mainly African American. The reported speech in her story is communicated through indirect discourse: "and sh- she said it couldn't, it hadn't occurred to her how hard it was for people in the circle . . . how hard it was to get diagnostic, diagnosis and care and so forth." Next, she ties my words to the broader contexts of health disparities and the event where she will perform the following day. Her story ends with a question directed to me: "but it was like, [*laughs, looking back at me*] you didn't know that, huh?"

This final line carries a kind of ambiguity, in that it is not quite clear to which frame the question belongs. Did she ask me that question at the time of the earlier story circle, or was it a new query, set in the frame of the present story circle? If the latter, who was the primary audience for that question? Me? The other participants in the story circle? She looked at me when she asked it, but as soon as she finished, another person immediately began a story about her own experiences, using the transitional phrase, "speaking of disparities"—indicating that McCauley's story about me, like the one shared by the woman before her, offered an example of factors contributing to African American health inequities.

The focus of McCauley's story is an instance of reported speech through indirect discourse, and I am the central character. Drawing upon the work of Deborah Tannen (1989) and Amy Shuman (1992) on the dynamic interrelationship between reported speech and the reporting frame, Gabriella Modan shows that "[t]hrough this relationship between the reported and reporting frames, speakers can take certain stances vis-à-vis the content or the utterer of the reported speech" (2007, 178). As I will show in the discussion below, McCauley's use of reported speech—along with its connection to my embodied presence—worked to call critical attention to the processes by which African American health disparities remain unquestioned.

During the same period of time in which I was transcribing my recording of this story circle, I read the script of McCauley's 1994 performance piece *Sally's Rape*, enacted by McCauley and Jeannie Hutchinson, which deals with the experiences of McCauley's great-great grandmother, a slave who had two children by one of her overseers. As I read this script, I saw myself—and more specifically, the way that McCauley had responded to my embodied, white self—in the character of Jeannie. Under the section entitled "Players," the character Jeannie is described as "the one who plays the roles she's given and who sometimes erupts. She is a dancer who sings and acts. She is white" (1994, 218). While a great deal of the piece consists of Jeannie playing herself and having conversations with Robbie onstage, she also slips in and out of playing other white characters, including Thomas Jefferson's wife, a slave dealer, and a white rape victim. Below is a section of the script in which Jeannie slips into and out of the persona of another white character:

Robbie [R]: In 1964 at the library job a US history major who'd graduated from Smith College said-

Jeannie [J]: I never knew white men did anything with colored women on plantations.

R: I said, "It was rape." Her eyes turned red. She choked on her sandwich and quit the job.

J: [*Pointing at each audience group in turn*] Was the Smith
    College graduate denying . . . ? lying? or dumb? [*Audience
    response*] Yeah, she was dumb. I keep telling you that.

In this scene, the words of the Smith College graduate are channeled
through the embodied presence of Jeannie. While she only takes on
this persona for one line, distancing herself from the Smith College
graduate the next time she speaks, the statement and what it represents—denial, lying, and/or stupidity—are intertwined with the
visual image of her marked white body.[17]

Theatre scholars have examined in detail McCauley's uses of the
body onstage and have identified the ways in which her body is a primary mode of communication in her performance pieces (Nymann
1999; Whyte 1993). According to Whyte, "[McCauley's] is at once a
body saturated with memories of sensual experience, a text written by
racism and bounded by family, history, and gender" (1993, 277). After
reading this play, I began to think about how the scene would have been
different if McCauley had been onstage by herself, if the audience had
not had the visual cue of Jeannie's body to ground the statement as a
marker of particularly *white* denial, lying, or stupidity. In this scene, and
in fact this whole play, the audience must engage visually with the
racialized bodies onstage as they engage with the racial issues being
addressed by the actors. The way Jeannie's body channels different
types of discourses calls attention to the ways in which discourses are
situated within and emergent from physical bodies.

I see at least one significant similarity between Jeannie and myself:
our marked physical bodies became communicative resources both
amidst and within our respective contexts, the dialogues taking place
on stage and in the story circle. In both cases, McCauley tied reported
speech to physical bodies that were present in the immediate performance contexts; she tied the words of the Smith College graduate to
Jeannie's body, and my past words to my embodied presence in the
reporting context. The visibility of Jeannie's body and my own allowed
certain things to go unsaid at the level of language (e.g., "She was
white"), while other positioning characteristics that were not visible
were specifically identified (e.g., "a US History major who'd graduated
from Smith College," "Sheila was helping the person responsible,"
"Sheila also has diabetes").

Thinking about McCauley's story in relation to the scene from *Sally's Rape*, I began to recognize the role played by my physical body, one in which the lines between reported and reporting contexts converged, past conversations were brought to bear on the present moment, and the immediate performance context was connected to larger social structures. McCauley drew on my present body—one marked as both white and diabetic—as a communicative resource in the reporting context; she used my words to demonstrate the types of (denying, lying, or dumb) discourses that contribute to, or at least naturalize the presence of, health disparities.

"Come on, Sheila. Come live on the Near East Side!"

McCauley returned to Columbus in March 2009 to conduct two more story circles; she also performed *Sugar* at the Department of African American and African Studies (AAAS) Community Extension Center located on the Near East Side. One participant in one of these story circles was Bill Thompson, a community resident actively engaged in fighting health issues within the African American community of central Ohio.[18] After McCauley's visit in March 2009, I contacted Thompson, along with several other story circle participants; I described my research project and asked them if they would be willing to talk to me about their thoughts on McCauley's performances and story circles. Thompson was one of those who graciously agreed to talk with me, and we made arrangements to meet at his house on a Saturday afternoon. When I showed up, several visitors were sitting in his living room. He introduced me to them and to his wife, explaining that I was there to talk about McCauley's performances. As they said goodbye to one another, he invited me to sit on the couch. When I asked permission to audio-record our conversation, he responded, "Oh! So this is a SERIOUS interview!" He then agreed and, as I pressed the record button on my small digital recorder sitting on the coffee table between us, he said, "So, Sheila, what would you like to know?"

I began by asking Thompson about his impressions of the performances, as well as how they might contribute to the kind of community work he was already doing. He replied:

Bill Thompson [BT]:
Sheila, I tend to speak with a voice that deals with issues of African Americans and health ((Sheila Bock [SB]: Mmhmm)) because everybody else deals with their particular concerns ((SB: yeah)) and the African American voice as it relates to chronic disease is really underrepresented ((SB: yeah)) and what I think that people like Robbie and people like myself do is bring a lot of attention to chronic disease that affects African Americans, not minorities ((SB: Mmhmm)) but African Americans, because when you look at the conditions of chronic disease like diabetes, African Americans are the leaders in terms of the prevalence of the disease, and the morbidity and the mortality of the disease. It's the worst thing, you know, when you deal with cardiovascular, diabetes, stroke, cancer, and all those categories African American people have the highest rate, ((SB: yeah)) you know, and it's not a minority issue, it's an African American issue, we all are affected by those diseases ((SB: yeah)) but the prevalence and the comorbidity factor is highest among African American people ((SB: yeah)).

I then asked, "You had mentioned during the story circle your part in getting the Near Eastside Healthy Lifestyle Center started, so those were the types of issues you were interested in addressing, right?" He began to tell me how his own diagnosis with type 2 diabetes led him to become involved in community health issues, and he explained how his own experiences showed him the importance of spreading the word in the community:

I was able to kind of think about and look at the research that had taken place that involved lifestyle changes. And there is nothing in the black community that supports healthy lifestyle living. All the messages you see, if you go down five, six blocks you'll see cigarettes and you'll see hard alcohol advertised, but you don't see anything in the African American community that speaks to living healthy . . . My argument has always been [that] for a suburban community, the infrastructure for being healthy is already built into that area, that you have grocery stores that have cooking classes, that you have schools and rec centers that promote physical activities and that there is a health tax for people who live in urban communities because we don't have those same infrastructures in place, so you know I tell anybody it's not that black folks are not predisposed to being healthy, it's that if I bring white folks in the urban setting with what's not here, they'll be unhealthy, too. And so the issue is that if you look at the urban setting, the impact is on people of color because that's where they reside. But if, you know, I wouldn't necessarily promote, this area here has the highest diabetes rate in the state. "Come on, Sheila, come live on the Near East Side!" You'd be like, [*shaking his head*] "No, Bill!" [*laughs*] and so those kinds of issues are issues that have to be addressed.

In this interaction, Thompson calls attention to the external forces (rather than internal attributes) that cause widespread rates of diabetes among African Americans. Like McCauley, he incorporates reported speech—"Come on, Sheila, come live on the Near East Side!" "No, Bill!"—into this discursive response to stigma. This rhetorical move, however, differs from McCauley's in at least one significant way. Thompson makes no claim that the event he describes has actually happened. Rather, he quotes from an imagined, hypothetical conversation. In the process, he demonstrates how speech reported using direct discourse is less a matter of faithful representation and more a "constructed dialogue" meant to comment upon the present communicative context (Tannen 1989, 103).

This hypothetical exchange, in fact, highlighted for me a convergence of personal and political modes: Thompson shaped his words to position himself in relation to me in a situated encounter; at the same time, he used imagined dialogue to prove a broader point about how structural inequalities shape health disparities. The me 'quoted' in his speech recognizes and shuns those structural and physical differences. Alessandro Portelli reports a similar discursive strategy in an oral history interview with Reverend Hugh and Mrs. Julia Cowan, an African American couple from Harlan County, Kentucky. In that interview, Mrs. Cowan said, "[A]lthough you might not have done a thing in this world to me, but because you're white, of what my parents said . . . I don't trust you, you know . . . There's gonna always be a line." Thoughtfully reflecting on this interaction, Portelli writes:

> In saying, "I don't trust you," she is ostensibly, and perhaps intentionally, speaking in general terms, using the impersonal *you*. But I could not help feeling that this broad, political mode was indissolubly twined with a very personal, immediate mode: she was talking in general, but she was also talking to me. (1997, 37; italics in original)

The metaphoric line invoked by Mrs. Cowan has a literal form in Thompson's discussion: it is a geographical boundary that separates

the Near East Side from other parts of Columbus, structures different
lifestyles, and has very real health implications.

The more I reflect upon Bill Thompson's words, the more I see
similarities between them and the rhetorical moves made by Robbie
McCauley in the story circle I describe above. What we see in both
encounters is not stigma management, as Goffman discusses, but
rather a critical engagement with stigma as a process rather than
merely an outcome. In these examples from my fieldwork, McCauley
and Thompson do not respond directly to explicitly stigmatizing language such as that employed by the surgeon. Rather, they communicate an underlying understanding that stigma is not merely a product
of sinister intentions, but a process in which I—along with other members of the category I represent—have been complicit.

It is important to acknowledge here that in both of these instances,
my body indexed a particular subjectivity that extended beyond race
and entered into issues of class as well. Obesity and its resulting health
issues are prevalent among white working-class people who also find
themselves in stigmatizing storylines.[19] When my whiteness is implicitly
invoked in the examples I present here, I am constructed as the other
on many levels, including those based on class, neighborhood, and
affiliation with the university. In these encounters, then, I am explicitly
marked as the unmarked, as one who does not find herself the subject
of stigmatizing storylines. Ultimately, then, through multiple framings,
I am engaged with as both an embodied presence and a discursive
category, an audience member and a communicative resource. As a
result, it has become impossible for me to look at others' situated
responses to the processes of stigma formation and maintenance without considering my own role in shaping those processes.

Contextualization and Methodological Reflexivity

Encountering myself in the performances described above has contributed to my understanding of both the rhetorical strategies people
employ to challenge stigmatizing storylines and the broader discursive
forces that keep these storylines in place. At the same time, attending to
the practices of contextualization in these performances has led me to
attend more critically to yet another form of contextualization in my
research and analysis: methodological reflexivity. Since the "reflexive
turn" in ethnographic disciplines, scholars have generally agreed that

fieldworkers need to be mindful of how their practices of fieldwork, interpretation, and representation shape their understandings of field data.[20] However, the term has come under scrutiny by scholars examining power dynamics embedded in and emerging from fieldwork encounters and their representations. Wanda Pillow, for example, looks critically at "the role of reflexivity as a methodological tool as it intersects with debates and questions surrounding representation and legitimization in qualitative research" (2003, 176). She joins others in questioning the link between reflexivity and 'better' research and the assumptions underlying its use as a methodological tool. One of Pillow's critiques is that self-reflexivity is often framed as a kind of "confession," allowing the researcher to present a "catharsis of self-awareness" that is presented unproblematically as a solution to the problems of representation (181). In other words, the hypervisibility of the researcher in her presentation of her fieldwork can actually work to obscure and perpetuate the unequal power relations shaping fieldwork encounters, even while purporting to do the opposite.

Pillow's critiques of reflexivity intersect in interesting ways with the work of Charles Briggs, who asserts that "[w]e cannot relegate the politics of scholarship to some peripheral realm of 'reflexive' inquiry, to excuse business-as-usual research from the task of examining the social and political underpinnings of the terms and contexts of its uses" (1993, 388). While Briggs focuses on how the metadiscursive construction of invisibility naturalizes the scholar's textual authority,[21] key points of his argument also extend to the hypervisibility of the researcher created through practices of self-reflexivity. Briggs explains that a scholar's authority in representations of fieldwork is based on a clear distinction between texts and contexts, and he identifies specific problems with the common tendency to approach texts and contexts as separate categories of analysis. His critique of the text/context divide— a divide especially relevant to the methodological exercise of reflexivity—is that categorically separating the two "makes it possible to avoid dealing with race, gender, social class, politics, history, or whatever other considerations one may wish to exclude" (407), subsequently making it possible to hide the power dynamics informing and emerging from the research process.

While their arguments focus on different modes of scholarly representation, both Pillow and Briggs illuminate how the authority of a scholar's interpretations depends very heavily on a text/context divide. Bringing Pillow's and Briggs's ideas together reveals that when reflexivity is used as a methodological practice, it becomes an exercise in which key elements of the context are constructed by the researcher. Put another way, situating reflexivity as a methodological exercise reifies distinctions between (1) the texts scholars represent and analyze, and (2) their contexts as frameworks of interpretation. The scholar situates herself in the domain of context, and audiences understand this context to be a framework for more clearly comprehending the topic of research. Consequently, this text/context divide makes it possible to differentiate the interpretive work *we* (scholars) do and the interpretive work *they* (the people we study) do, sorting scholarly-interpretations and vernacular interpretations into separate, hierarchically ordered categories of analysis.

Like both Pillow and Briggs, however, I do not think that fieldworkers should stop considering and writing about the roles they play in the research process. I also acknowledge that the representations of my fieldwork encounters in this chapter have been heavily shaped by my own attempts at thoughtful self-reflexivity, and thus are not exempt from the critiques I present here. But in offering my own reflexive engagement in the previous pages not as models to follow but as examples that are useful to "think with," I join Briggs, Pillow, and other scholars in calling for increased critical attention to the assumptions underlying our work as researchers.

The discursive moves of scholarly differentiation and ranking can be especially problematic when working with stigmatized groups and individuals. Stigma, after all, results from the construction and maintenance of boundaries between those who are stigmatized and those who are not. As I discussed earlier, diabetes-related stigma occurs as the outcome of a process stemming from structures of inequality that extend well beyond the particular times and spaces in which people experience stigma at the individual level. As such, intervention in this process needs to involve strategies for disrupting the discursive mechanisms by which these structures of inequality are naturalized and remain unquestioned. In the process of offering their own interpretations and analyses structured by the text/context divide, researchers may frame the performances of stigmatized individuals more as expressive objects than as spaces of interpretation and critique, thereby running a very real risk of devaluing the authority of these perspectives. Such mechanisms of devaluation can consequently contribute to broader discursive forces keeping power differentials and stigmatizing storylines in place.

Even though I sought to take my analysis beyond a simple text/context divide by identifying strategies of contextualization in the performances I encountered, my attempts to situate my own role in these encounters were structured by this very same divide. I initially situated the performers' reflexivity in the domain of text, while I understood my own self-reflexivity to be in the domain of context. Had I not encountered performed characterizations of myself—characterizations that blurred any clear-cut boundary between these two domains of analysis—I do not know if I would have recognized that this foundational assumption structured my research.

As it happened, seeing myself performed by my interlocutors led me to some insights about the relationships between the performers' goals and my own. McCauley, Thompson, and I all seek to call into question the stigmatizing storylines associated with diabetes. We realize that stigma emerges from very specific contexts, and we understand these contexts to be constituted at the level of discourse and thus open to change. In our efforts to contribute to such changes, we draw upon each other, transforming present bodies into discursive resources in our attempts to validate the legitimacy of our interpretations. The ways we have crafted interpretive frameworks for one another, however, do different types of work for the project of de-stigmatization. McCauley's and Thompson's contextualizing practices call attention to the larger structures of inequality that leave unquestioned the boundaries created during the process of stigmatization. Mine, unwittingly, may naturalize these same boundaries. However, as researchers, explicitly questioning the dichotomies structuring our scholarly engagement with stigmatized individuals and communities increases the likelihood that we will be able to participate more productively in the work of de-stigmatization.

Acknowledgments

First and foremost, I owe many thanks to Robbie McCauley, Bill Thompson, and all the other individuals who generously shared their time and insights with me during the course of my research. I am also grateful to Dorothy Noyes, Diane Goldstein, Amy Shuman, Katherine Borland, and Ann Ferrell for their feedback and encouragement while I worked on this chapter. Finally, thank you to the editors and the anonymous reviewer, whose thoughtful comments and suggestions helped me refine the various strands of the argument presented here.

Notes

1. When a person is first diagnosed with diabetes, health professionals often ask that person to change his or her dietary habits radically. Because food is often central to expressing social and individual identities, prescribed food choices have the potential to interfere with a newly diagnosed patient's social world and sense of self (Ferzacca 2004; Jones 2007).

2. For examples of scholarly works that examine diabetes narratives, see Garro 1995, 2006; Garro and Lang 1993; Lang 1989, 2006; and Smith-Morris 2006.

3. Berger and Del Negro draw upon the works of Barbara Babcock (1980, 1987) and Richard Bauman (1989) in presenting these different (though related) contexts in which scholars use the term *reflexivity*.

4. Gestational diabetes is another form of the disease; it occurs temporarily during pregnancy for some women. Although this form is temporary, women with gestational diabetes are more likely to develop type 2 diabetes later in life.

5. These comments on Parker-Pope's article (2009) were posted online by Donna Handy (August 4, 2009, 7:30 p.m.), Charles (August 5, 2009, 11:29 a.m.), and Marv Golden (August 5, 2009, 12:18 p.m.).

6. For an insightful analysis of the interplay of medicalization, common sense, and the emergence of a folk tradition, see Heimerdinger 2011.

7. Indeed, her response resonates with philosopher George Yancy's words in *Black Bodies, White Gazes: The Continuing Significance of Race.* "From the perspective of whiteness, the Black body *is* criminality itself" (2008, xvi; italics his).

8. I would like to thank the anonymous reviewer for helping me articulate this point.

9. For Goffman, "abominations of the body" refers to physical deformities; "blemishes of individual character" to invisible flaws such as weak will; and "tribal stigma" to membership in stigmatized groups.

10. See Briggs 2005, Briggs and Mantini-Briggs 2003, and Goldstein 2001 for folkloristic examinations of similar issues.

11. A student of Johannes Fabian, Pool built upon Fabian's approach toward ethnography as a performative rather than an informative endeavor—that is, as a process in which meaning is produced rather than one in which preexisting information is accessed and documented (e.g., Fabian 1990). See also Sawin 2004 and Tedlock and Mannheim 1995 for discussions and demonstrations of the inherently dialogic and emergent nature of ethnographic endeavors.

12. The NEHLC has since closed due to funding cuts.

13. See Cieri and McCauley 2007 for a description of McCauley's use of and reflections on the story circle method.

14. For more in-depth examination of the performance piece *Sugar,* see Bock 2015 and chapter 2 of Carr 2007.

15. The hemoglobin A1c test measures a person's average blood glucose levels over an approximate three-month period. For people without diabetes, the normal range is 4.0–6.0%. For people with diabetes, the goal is less than 7.0%.

16. As the 2007 story circle session proceeded, several participants—particularly McCauley and staff members of the NEHLC—worked to tie individual experiences into a more 'collective' African American experience. For example, the "I" in McCauley's recounting of her own experiences slipped into a "we" when she said, "We [African Americans] are especially creative around spirituality." At another point during the circle, the conversation turned to physical activity levels among children: participants commented that today's kids were much less active than their peers in earlier decades. One woman recounted playing until dark and knowing it was time to come home when the street lights came on, and one of the health educators responded, "That's an African American home— when the street light comes on, you better come in!"

17. The phenotype of whiteness, then, indexes categorical characteristics of white subjectivity.

18. "Bill Thompson" is a pseudonym.

19. See Bock and Horigan (2015), pp. 73–79, for a discussion of diabetes related stigma experienced within the Appalachian community.

20. Folklorists have made valuable contributions to our understanding of the practical and theoretical issues of situating oneself and one's motives in the fieldwork encounter. See, for example, Lawless 1993, Nájera-Ramírez 1999, Paredes 1977, and Sawin 2004.

21. Briggs defines metadiscursive practices as "the methods used in locating, extracting, and interpreting various forms of discourse" (1993, 388). He focuses his discussion specifically on the ways folklore scholars attempt to present 'authentic' performances of the folk as spoken to the folk, "erasing the role of the scholar in the production of folkloric texts" (411). He argues that this rhetoric of authenticity depends on the constructed absence of the fieldworker, and that the metadiscursive practices creating the fieldworker's invisibility in the production of texts ultimately reinforce the researcher's scholarly authority, naturalizing the ability to speak about and on behalf of the performers and the performance texts being represented.

References

Babcock, Barbara. 1980. "Reflexivity: Definitions and Discriminations." *Semiotica* 30:1–14.

——. 1987. "Reflexivity." In *The Encyclopedia of Religion*, vol. 12, edited by Mircea Eliade, 234–38. New York: Macmillan.

Balshem, Martha. 1993. *Cancer in the Community: Class and Medical Authority.* Washington, DC: Smithsonian Institution Press.

Bateson, Gregory. 1972. *Steps to an Ecology of Mind: Collected Essays in Anthropology, Psychiatry, Evolution, and Epistemology.* Chicago: University of Chicago Press.

Bauman, Richard. 1989. "Performance." In *The International Encyclopedia of Performance*, edited by Erik Barnouw, 262–66. Oxford: Oxford University Press.

Bauman, Richard, and Charles L. Briggs. 1990. "Poetics and Performance as Critical Perspectives on Language and Social Life." *Annual Review of Anthropology* 19:59–88.

Berger, Harris M., and Giovanna P. Del Negro. 2002. "Bauman's *Verbal Art* and the Social Organization of Attention: The Role of Reflexivity in the Aesthetics of Performance." *Journal of American Folklore* 115 (455): 62–91.

Bock, Sheila. 2015. "Grappling to Think Clearly": Vernacular Theorizing in Robbie McCauley's Sugar. *Journal of Medical Humanities* 33: 127–139.

Bock, Sheila and Kate Parker Horigan. 2015. "Invoking the Relative: A New Perspective on Family Lore in Stigmatized Communities." In *Diagnosing Folklore: Perspectives on Health, Trauma, and Disability,* edited by Trevor J. Blank and Andrea Kitta, 65–84. Jackson: University Press of Mississippi.

Boero, Natalie. 2007. "All the News that's Fat to Print: The American 'Obesity Epidemic' and the Media." *Qualitative Sociology* 30 (1): 41–60.

Briggs, Charles L. 1993. "Metadiscursive Practices and Scholarly Authority in Folkloristics." *Journal of American Folklore* 106 (422): 387–434.

———. 2005. "Communicability, Racial Discourse, and Disease." *Annual Review of Anthropology* 34:269–91.

Briggs, Charles, and Clara Mantini-Briggs. 2003. *Stories in the Time of Cholera: Racial Profiling during a Medical Nightmare.* Berkeley and Los Angeles: University of California Press.

Broom, Dorothy, and Andrea Whittaker. 2004. "Controlling Diabetes, Controlling Diabetics: Moral Language in the Management of Diabetes Type 2." *Social Science and Medicine* 58:2371–82.

Campbell, Cathy, and Harriet Deacon. 2006. "Unravelling the Contexts of Stigma: From Internalisation to Resistance to Change." *Journal of Community & Applied Social Psychology* 16 (6): 411–17.

Carr, Tessa. 2007. "Recovering Women: Autobiographical Performances of Illness Experience." PhD diss., University of Texas, Austin.

Cieri, Marie, and Robbie McCauley. 2007. "Participatory Theatre: Creating a Source for Staging an Example in the USA." In *Participatory Action Research Approaches and Methods: Connecting People, Participation and Place,* edited by Sara Louise Kindon, 141–49. New York: Routledge.

Crawford, Robert. 1977. "You are Dangerous to Your Health: The Ideology and Politics of Victim Blaming." *International Journal of Health Services* 7 (4): 663–80.

———. 1980. "Healthism and the Medicalisation of Everyday Life." *International Journal of Health Services* 10:365–88.

Das, Veena. 2001. "Stigma, Contagion, Defect: Issues in the Anthropology of Public Health." http://www.stigmaconference.nih.gov/FinalDasPaper.htm.

Diabetes Fact Sheet. 2010. Columbus, OH: Ohio Department of Health. http://www.odh.ohio.gov/sitecore/content/HealthyOhio/default/diabetes/diadata.aspx.

Fabian, Johannes. 1990. *Power and Performance: Ethnographic Explorations through Proverbial Wisdom and Theater in Shaba, Zaire.* Madison: University of Wisconsin Press.

Ferrell, Ann. "'Replacing' Tobacco on Kentucky Farms: Discourses of Tradition, Heritage, and Agricultural Diversification." PhD diss., The Ohio State University, 2009.

Ferzacca, Steve. 2004. "Lived Food and Judgments of Taste at a Time of Disease." *Medical Anthropology* 23:41–67.

Garro, Linda C. 1995. "Individual or Societal Responsibility? Explanations of Diabetes in an Anishinaabe (Ojibway) Community." *Social Science and Medicine* 40 (1): 37–46.

———. 2006. "Talking about a New Illness with the Dakota: Reflections on Diabetes, Food, and Culture." In *Indigenous Peoples and Diabetes: Community Empowerment and Wellness,* edited by Mariana Leal Ferreira and Gretchen Chesley Lang, 203–30. Durham, NC: Carolina Academic Press.

Garro, Linda C., and Gretchen Chesley Lang. 1993. "Explanations of Diabetes: Anishinaabeg and Dakota Deliberate upon a New Illness." In *Diabetes as a Disease of Civilization: The Impact of Culture Change on Indigenous Peoples,* edited by Jenny Joe and Robert S. Young, 293–328. Berlin: Mouton de Gruyter.

Goffman, Erving. 1963. *Stigma: Notes on the Management of Spoiled Identity.* Englewood Cliffs, NJ: Prentice-Hall.

———. 1974. *Frame Analysis: An Essay on the Organization of Experience.* Cambridge, MA: Harvard University Press.

Goldstein, Diane E. 2001. "Competing Logics and the Construction of Risk." In *Healing Logics: Culture and Medicine in Modern Health Belief Systems,* edited by Erika Brady, 129–40. Logan: Utah State University Press.

Goodwin, Charles, and Alessandro Duranti, eds. 1992. *Rethinking Context: Language as an Interactive Phenomenon.* Cambridge: Cambridge University Press.

Gumperz, John. 1982. *Discourse Strategies.* Cambridge: Cambridge University Press.

———. 1992. "Contextualization and Understanding." In *Rethinking Context: Language as an Interactive Phenomenon,* edited by Alesandro Duranti and Charles Goodwin, 229–52. Cambridge: Cambridge University Press.

"Healthy Neighborhood Report: Near East." 2004. Columbus, OH: Columbus Health Department.

Heimerdinger, Timo. 2011. "Pacifiers and Fairies: Family Culture as Risk Management—A German Example." *Journal of Folklore Research* 48 (2): 197–211.

Howarth, Caroline. 2006. "Race as Stigma: Positioning the Stigmatized as Agents, Not Objects." *Journal of Community and Applied Social Psychology* 16 (6): 442–51.

Jones, Michael Owen. 2007. "Food Choice, Symbolism, and Identity: Bread-and-Butter Issues for Folkloristics and Nutrition Studies (2005 American Folklore Society Presidential Address)." *Journal of American Folklore* 120 (476): 129–77.

Kapchan, Deborah A. 1995. "Performance." *Journal of American Folklore* 108 (430): 479–508.

Lang, Gretchen Chesley. 1989. " 'Making Sense' About Diabetes: Dakota Narratives of Illness." *Medical Anthropology* 11:305–27.

———. 2006. "'In Their Tellings': Dakota Narratives about History and the Body." In *Indigenous Peoples and Diabetes: Community Empowerment and Wellness,* edited by Mariana Leal Ferreira and Gretchen Chesley Lang, 53–71. Durham, NC: Carolina Academic Press.

Lawless, Elaine J. 1993. *Holy Women, Wholly Women: Sharing Ministries of Wholeness through Life Stories and Reciprocal Ethnography.* Philadelphia: University of Pennsylvania Press.

Link, Bruce G., and Jo C. Phelan. 2001. "Conceptualizing Stigma." *Annual Review of Sociology* 27:363–85.

———. 2006. "Stigma and Its Public Health Implications." *Lancet* 367:528–9.

Lupton, Deborah. 1995. *The Imperative of Health: Public Health and the Regulated Body.* London: Sage.

Modan, Gabriella Gahlia. 2007. *Turf Wars: Discourse, Diversity, and the Politics of Place.* Malden, MA: Blackwell.

McCauley, Robbie. 1994. "Sally's Rape." In *Moon Marked and Touched By Sun: Plays by African-American Women,* edited by Sydné Mahone, 211–38. New York: Theatre Communications Group.

———. 2009. Interview by author, Columbus, OH. Audio Recording. March 12. Recording in possession of author.

Nájera-Ramírez, Olga. 1999. "Of Fieldwork, Folklore, and Festival: Personal Encounters." *Journal of American Folklore* 112 (444): 183–99.

"National Diabetes Fact Sheet: National Estimates and General Information on Diabetes and Pre-diabetes in the United States." 2011. Atlanta, GA: United States Department of Health and Human Services and Centers for Disease Control and Prevention.

Nymann, Ann E. 1999. "Sally's Rape: Robbie McCauley's Survival Art." *African American Review* 33 (4): 577–87.

Paredes, Américo. 1977. "On Ethnographic Work among Minority Groups: A Folklorist's Perspective." *Journal of Folklore Research* 25:145–54.

Parker-Pope, Tara. 2009. "The Voices of Type 2 Diabetes." *The New York Times,* August 4. http://well.blogs.nytimes.com/2009/08/04/the-voices-of-type-2-diabetes/.

Pillow, Wanda. 2003. "Confession, Catharsis, or Cure?: Rethinking the Uses of Reflexivity as Methodological Power in Qualitative Research." *Qualitative Studies in Education* 16 (2): 175–96.

Pool, Robert. 1994. *Dialogue and the Interpretation of Illness: Conversations in a Cameroon Village.* Oxford: Berg.

Portelli, Alessandro. 1997. *The Battle of Valle Giulia: Oral History and the Art of Dialogue.* Madison: University of Wisconsin Press.

Sawin, Patricia. 2004. *Listening for a Life: A Dialogic Ethnography of Bessie Eldreth through Her Songs and Stories.* Logan: Utah State University Press.

Saylor, Colleen R. 1990. "The Management of Stigma: Redefinition and Representation." *Holistic Nursing Practice* 5 (1): 45–53.

Shuman, Amy. 1992. "'Get Outa My Face': Entitlement and Authoritative Discourse." In *Responsibility and Evidence in Oral Discourse,* edited by Jane H. Hill and Judith T. Irvine, 135–60. Cambridge: Cambridge University Press.

Smith-Morris, Carolyn. 2006. *Diabetes among the Pima: Stories of Survival.* Tucson: University of Arizona Press.

Tannen, Deborah. (1989) 2006. *Talking Voices: Repetition, Dialogue, and Imagery in Conversational Discourse.* Cambridge: Cambridge University Press.
Tedlock, Dennis, and Bruce Mannheim, eds. 1995. *The Dialogic Emergence of Culture.* Urbana: University of Illinois Press.
Turner, Aaron. 2000. "Embodied Ethnography: Doing Culture." *Social Anthropology* 8:51–60.
Wailoo, Keith. 2006. "Stigma, Race, and Disease in 20th-Century America." *Lancet* 367:533–34.
Whyte, Raewyn. 1993. "Robbie McCauley: Speaking History Other-wise." In *Acting Out: Feminist Performances,* edited by Lynda Hart and Peggy Phelan, 277–93. Ann Arbor: University of Michigan Press.
Yancy, George. 2008. *Black Bodies, White Gazes: The Continuing Significance of Race.* Plymouth, UK: Rowman and Littlefield.

SHEILA BOCK is Assistant Professor of Interdisciplinary Studies at the University of Nevada, Las Vegas. Her research interests include the contested domains of illness experience, performance and differential identity, foodways, the intersections between folklore and popular culture, and the multivocality of ethnographic research.

3 Rethinking Ventriloquism: Untellability, Chaotic Narratives, Social Justice, and the Choice to Speak For, About, and Without

REPRESENTATIONAL POLITICS IN folklore have continually emphasized the inclusion of multiple voices in our published texts, as well as the need to find more and better mechanisms to let underrepresented voices be heard. Over the years our strategies of representation have been criticized, however, for focusing on the integration of marginal voices by sometimes choosing to speak on behalf of underrepresented communities, rather than letting them speak for themselves. In an excellent critique of representational politics in folklore—one modeled on Spivak's (1988) "Can the Subaltern Speak?"—Susan Ritchie writes about the folklorist as "ventriloquist," or one who presumes "to speak on behalf of some voiceless group or individual" (1993, 366). Ventriloquism, she writes, establishes "the folklorist as a kind of medium or channeler, who presents the true voices of those otherwise lost to an audience so eager for diverse articulations that they fail to note [that] this 'diversity'. . . issues from a single disciplinary throat" (367). Ritchie cautions us about imagined mutism and agency, questioning the sometimes naive notion that fieldwork-based representation is always a universal good, while ignoring attention to what can happen to previously local expressions when they are catapulted into larger discourses. Ritchie's concern is with two issues: first, "that informants maintain control and ownership of their performances . . . within the final work," and second, "that the presentation of the folklorist's object of study remains entirely consistent with the individual performer's self-presentation" (367). Nowhere are Ritchie's cautions more relevant than in those complex situations in which, as a result of our informants' already stig-matized identities or lack of discursive competence, self-representation or even collaborative representation is likely to serve only to deepen and strengthen power differentials.

This chapter will explore the reflexive challenges presented by the intersection of stigma, untellability, and social justice, as well as how this intersection necessitates making complex decisions about how to represent the chaotic voices of vulnerable research subjects. I begin by recounting an interaction that made me question my decision to publish a chaotic narrative. I then sketch out concepts of chaotic narrative and untellability. In subsequent sections, I draw from pub-lished accounts of trauma and chaotic narrative in order to discuss how chaos and untellability manifest themselves in narrative: as inef-fability, as fragmentation, as disassociation, and as devaluation. My primary concern in this chapter is with our ability to be empathetic to the effects of trauma on narrative coherence and to identify those occasions when the choice to speak for, about, or without the voices of individuals in our study might be the most appropriate decision.

Confronting Chaos and the Effects of Ventriloquism

In autumn 2008, I was invited by Peggy Yocum to speak at "Fall for the Book," a literary festival held each year at George Mason University.[1] Peggy asked me to speak about *Once Upon a Virus*(2004), my book on AIDS legends and vernacular risk perception. Chapter six (116–38) of the book provides an ethnographic study of the legal and community narrative construction of a criminal case involving Ray Mercer, a Newfoundland man tried and found guilty of "deliberate infection with HIV." As I explored the discursive construction of this case—focusing on the vernacular and official narratives that turned Ray into a public health scapegoat—I worked hard to make the chapter as multi-vocal as possible by including the voices and narratives of community members, police officers, lawyers, judges, media representatives, public health workers, the forensic psychiatrist, the Red Cross, the victims, and the accused. During the question-and-answer session that followed my talk, an audience member who had read my book commented that although she was sensitive to the stigmatization and scapegoating of one individ-ual, Mercer's own words—as presented in the book—had convinced her that he was, in fact, demented.

I was a little taken aback. While it stands to reason that a man who knowingly infected two women with HIV might be completely mad, Ray was not, and I had worked hard in my writing to contextualize that fact. Understood locally as 'slow,' Ray was mentally challenged and had only a fourth-grade education. He continually asserted that he felt fine and wasn't sick at all. Though Ray was found guilty of knowingly infecting two women, he had clearly demonstrated to the forensic psychiatrist involved in the case that he didn't understand what it was to be HIV positive, especially as it pertained to his 'healthy carrier' status. I was disturbed by the interpretation of the student at the George Mason event—but I was even more disturbed when I re-read the words I had quoted, the ones that provided Ray's account of the events leading up to his eventual conviction. I could see that his comments were chaotic, suggesting unpredictability, imbalance, and perhaps even malevolence. I felt suddenly that I had misrepresented Ray—and that I had done so by quoting *his own* self-representation. Ray said, and I quoted (using punctuation and spelling from the original statement):

> Raymond Mercer is a 29-year-old resident of Upper Island Cove, Nfld., Canada. In July 1992 the defendant pleaded guilty to two charges of having unprotected sex with two women, knowingly being HIV pos. The facts in the case is that these two women stated they were HIV pos also. Therefore what harm could come of people who are HIV positive having sex with one another. Charge number one <u>Susan</u>. Here is a girl I met in a night club in Harbour Grace the Piarts Cave. So naturally you assume that a person is nineteen years old to be in a club. Not so then to find out that this girl was sixteen at the time leave me to believe that I am being used as a scape goat in this case. This girl knew I was HIV pos at the time. So where are the facts in this case by the Crown that I infected her with this virus. Can Susan prove that I Raymond Mercer infected her with this virus. (Goldstein 2004, 129)

Ray's account of the events is disjointed, unintelligible in some places, and chaotic. He jumps from one issue to another, uses pretend legalese, and mixes up deliberate infection with the issue of having sex with a minor—an issue that never appeared in the police reports or the charges. But Ray's account also came about in an unusual way. When Ray made this statement he was incarcerated on the mainland of Canada. Because of my involvement in the case as an expert witness, I was instructed by the lawyers not to visit or interview Ray, which meant relying on Ray's written comments. Unable to read or write due to his intellectual challenges, Ray had dictated his account to a fellow prison inmate.

The account is thus mediated in a number of ways: by the written mode, by the constraints of incarceration, by the transcription of Ray's jailhouse buddy, and by my editorial choices as an ethnographer. I included Ray's account in the book because I couldn't imagine *not* including his voice in a chapter about him, and because understanding his perspective on the issues was clearly central to my discussion. But the more I thought about the comment from the woman at George Mason, the more I wondered about what I had done—my choices, my motives, and the end result. If the chaos of Ray's narrative conjured up images of a crazy person—rather than invoking the intellectually challenged, scapegoated, and demonized individual I saw in surrounding narrative and forensic evidence—hadn't quoting that narrative done him a disservice, rather than a service? Was Ray best able to represent himself and his own perspectives—as Ritchie suggests—or did he, in fact, need a ventriloquist? I wanted to empower Ray by representing his voice, and yet I seemed to have accomplished exactly the opposite.

The more I thought about the situation, the more the issues intrigued me. I had wanted Ray's voice to be there, not only to represent his perspective—which, admittedly, I might have done better—but also to *actualize* him, to make him a fact. From a kind perspective (that is, one kind to me as decision maker), we could say that my inclusion of Ray's account humanizes him, making this stigmatized, demonized individual real in the face of the fictionalized narrative version of him constructed by justice officials, public health workers, and the local community. From a not-so-kind (to me) critical point of view, my inclusion of his narrative objectifies him. Ray's testimony, chaotic or not, is evidence of his ethnographic existence, evidence that one needs to have in order to persuade readers that an ethnographic account is both authentic and authoritative.[2] And yet, as Margaret Mills reminds us, quoting James Clifford,

> while there is "liberation . . . in recognizing that no one can write about others any longer as if they were discrete objects or texts" (Clifford 1986, 25), . . . "giving a voice" itself is highly problematical, hardly empowering; "plural authorship" remains a "utopia," and the "authoritative stance of 'giving voice' to the other is not totally transcended" (Clifford 1988, 51).

One cannot stand clear out of the way while the other speaks, because one *is* the "way." (1991, 16)

Chaotic Narratives and Untellability

Ray's chaotic narrative is complicated by the nature of his crime, a crime so demonized and so stigmatized that it does not easily evoke sympathetic response. But chaotic narratives are not uncommon, and even in situations that evoke great sympathy—those that are deeply violent and traumatic, those in which the narrator is more clearly a victim/survivor and not a perpetrator—the chaos threatens to misrepresent narrators, further silencing their perspectives and the articulation of experience.

I use *chaotic narratives* here to refer to those narratives that lack an apparent order or organization and that are unpredictable and confusing. As McAdams argues with respect to what he calls "coherent narratives," "stories that defy structural expectations about time, intention, goal, causality, or closure may . . . strike audiences as incoherent, or at least incomplete" (2006, 111).[3] Clearly, we would tread dangerous ground if we were understood to be specifying a universal narrative aesthetic of structure, plot, expectation, or chronology (e.g., Heath 1983). Nevertheless, narratives and narrators *are* governed and constrained by local norms of coherence, norms that assume competence for satisfying audience expectations regarding structure, order, form, and content. Narration understood by audiences as chaotic can take many forms, including but not limited to 1) performances produced prior to competence acquisition, as might be found in young children or new culture members; 2) performances resulting from different cultural aesthetics; 3) the performance of purposeful incoherence directed at specific ends and goals; 4) performances in which consciousness or performance capacity is altered by drugs or alcohol; 5) inability to articulate coherency due to health or intellectual challenge; and 6) ineffability or inarticulateness due to traumatic experience. Because an assessment of narrative chaos can easily suggest a clash in narrative aesthetics or worldview, I reserve my use of the term *chaotic* for situations in which narrative confusion, fragmentation, or disorder is the result of traumatic, psychological, or intellectual challenge; where it results in an inability to articulate experience;

and/or where the chaos of the experience itself becomes larger than any narrative can handle. Violent and traumatic experiences, as well as mental and cognitive challenges, frequently result in deep untellability (e.g., Goldstein 2009; Labov and Waletzky 1967; Lawless 2001; Norrick 2005; Sacks 1992; Shuman 2006; Shuman and Bohmer 2004; Wycoff 1996), a state in which narratives of experience become fragmented, incoherent, and chaotic, if articulated at all. Narratives of rape (Bletzer and Koss 2004; Hesford 1999), domestic violence (Howell 2004; Lawless 2001), and war and natural disaster (Huynh Chau Nguyen 2008; Nordstrom and Robben 1995), as well as those associated with Alzheimer's (Ramanathan 1995), severe learning disabilities (Booth and Booth 1996), agoraphobia (Capps and Ochs 1995), and developmental delay (Medved 2004) have all been discussed in relation to untellability and the silencing or degenerative chaos-producing effect on personal narrative.

Based on the way Sacks (1992) and Labov and Waletzky (1967) use the concept of *tellability* or *speakability* as a crucial requisite for competent narration manifest in speaker and audience assessments of relevance, importance, newsworthiness, appropriateness, and entitlement, I use the term *untellability* here to refer to limited comfort or ability of the narrator because of perceived restrictions of *context*— such as narrator interpretations of discursive safety or risk—as well as issues of *content* arising from faulty memory, confusion, fragmentation, and an inability to articulate. The chaotic narratives discussed here might be, on the surface, most easily understood as unwriteable, rather than untellable; in other words, the chaos is most apparent as the text moves from oral to written form. In written texts—as we commit narrative to the page—linearity, fragmentation, silences, and disorder become all the more apparent.[4] But many chaotic texts do not depend on writing to reveal their chaotic nature; rather, they are experienced and received as chaotic at the time of performance. While the example from Ray (above) concerns the outsider's assessment of chaos and the external reception of narrative, often both narrator and audience perceive chaos arising out of deep and complex untellability. Untellability in this sense resides in both discourse and experience.[5] Exploring both chaotic narrative and reported narrator *experience* of traumatic untellability will hopefully provide empathetic insight into the many challenges people face in articulating the untellable and suggest points for thinking and making decisions about how best to represent the chaotic and the untellable in our scholarly research.

Ineffability

Trauma sometimes results in an inability to put words to experience, rendering narrative coherence untenable. Writing about the Holocaust, for example, Roberta Culbertson remarks on the ineffability of violent memories. She asks,

> If violence leaves memories of wounding and transcendence that for different reasons have little connection with language, then how can so-called memory be communicated? How can we—survivors and non-survivors alike—come to know anything about violence and its effects if we encounter fundamental difficulties in describing those effects? (1995, 178–79)

Culbertson argues that victims "cannot make the leap to words," that there are no words "to describe the nightmare," and that one cannot express trauma to "someone who never knew that such a degree of brutality" exists. Like so many who write or speak about traumatic memory, she describes the narrator's experience of articulation as a struggle with ineffability. The demands of narrative operate as cultural silencers, Culbertson argues, because "wordless language is unintelligible to one whose body is not similarly affected" (170).

Ineffability is well documented in the scholarly literature on trauma and narrative. Arthur Frank, for instance, claims that chaotic narratives are incompatible with writing and telling: "Those who are truly *living* the chaos cannot tell [it] in words. . . . The chaos that can be told in story is already taking place at a distance and is being reflected on retrospectively. . . . Lived chaos makes reflection and consequently story-telling impossible" (1995, 97–98; italics in original). Elaine Lawless agrees. Writing about women's narratives of domestic violence, she observes,

> [T]here is a point where acute violence enters and where the narrative appears to break down, where language and words, apparently, cannot do justice to the pain and the violations, where the narrative becomes erratic, loses its coherence, and resists failure by deferring to silence in order to do the event justice. (2001, 64)

And writing about pain, Elaine Scarry argues that "[i]ntense pain is . . . language destroying: as the content of one's world disintegrates, so the content of one's language disintegrates; as the self disintegrates, so that which would express and project the self is robbed of its source and its subject" (1985, 35). Chaotic and untellable narratives are chaotic and untellable precisely because the nature of trauma makes the narrator unable to put experience to words. Trauma affects the self in such a way as to make coherence impossible, at least temporarily.

Fragmentation and the Non-linear Nature of Traumatic Memory

Ineffability can play a large part in narrative chaos, so, too, does the nature of traumatic memory, which clinicians consistently observe is characterized by fragmentary and intense sensations, often with little or no verbal narrative content (Van der Kolk, Hopper, and Osterman 2001, 9). While traumatic memories might appear in non-narrative flashbacks, other parts of traumatic events disappear altogether. These lacunae present continual problems in linear articulation for those in legal advocacy situations, who assist victims/survivors in reconstructing legal narratives for prosecution of perpetrators—or, as Shuman and Bohmer (2004) report, to support refugee claims of homeland persecution when seeking asylum. Cathy Winkler, who wrote frankly and movingly about her own rape, notes with confusion parts of the event that she traumatically forgot or from which she had disassociated. She writes:

> When the rapist had initially swung wide in his attempts to batter me, he had hit the lamp and broken the bulb. The splattered particles of the bulb fell over the bed, and the rapist had pushed my back for hours into those bits of splinted glass that had fallen onto the bed covers. No pain existed for me. After arriving at the hospital, I still had no idea of the condition of my back. During the examination, the doctor noted that she would have to remove the glass particles before sewing up my back. I asked, "Why?" (Winkler and Hanke 1995, 173)

Flashbacks, along with scattered memories and forgettings, also threaten the coherence of her narrative. Winkler goes on to ask:

> Did the rapist and I talk on the subway a month and a half before the attack? I remember the rapist putting on a baseball cap the same way a stranger who spoke to me on the subway did and they were both people

who use drugs. Did he try to break into my home earlier but gave it up because I received a late night phone call? Why couldn't I remember the day of that telephone call and who made it? Why did he rape me?

(173)

The fragmentation of this narrative—brought on by the trauma of the rape itself—is plainly evident, as Winkler jumps from one thought to another. I recall a friend who, like Winkler, was raped many years ago. Speaking to her almost immediately after the rape, I could hardly follow her story, which, like Winkler's, was continually dotted with fragmentary images and questions: "and then he grabbed me—his hands—something odd about his hands—a birthmark?— tattoo?— strong cologne—did I hit him?—blood pouring into my eye—mine or his?—did I scream?"

Fragmentary narratives, though a natural part of the coping and sense-making process of victims, sometimes threaten their own coherence and reception. In a discussion of her own sexual assault, philosopher Susan Brison (2002) writes in a style designed to reflect the sporadic, confusing, fragmented forms of traumatic narration. Commenting on Brison's book, Susan Hirsh observes that "with respect to the problem of voice, the writing is fascinating and technically brilliant, but it makes for a difficult read. Ironically, the challenge to readers comes equally from the story's painful subject matter and the excruciating partial narrative patterns of a trauma victim's storytelling" (2007, 169). Although the stylistic use of fragmentation mirrors lived experience, making trauma real, the fragmentation also renders narrative chaotic and difficult for audiences to follow.

Although some evidence exists that chaotic narratives—dotted with flashbacks and seemingly random images—settle down over time, becoming more linear, they also appear, at least for some narrators, to fragment again when the teller is faced with traumatic moments of remembering. Hirsh, who was a surviving victim of the 1998 United States Embassy bombings in Dar es Salaam—and who lost her husband in the attacks—wrote about re-experiencing the fragmentation of images and words during legal hearings about the event:

[W]hen the testimony turned to eyewitness accounts of what happened in the Dar es Salaam bombing as reported by victims, my notes changed dramatically. I wrote and wrote, as fast as witnesses spoke, taking down just fragments, one to each line: "gunfire," "went to Emb—then back," "Marines have secured the building," "glass in my braids." Read back, the scribbles make little sense. That they resemble some of the writing I did right after the bombing is not surprising as hearing the eyewitness stories took me directly back to those moments of severe shock and grief. (2007, 157)

Disassociation and the Threat of Perceived Imbalance

So often though, chaotic narrative is more than fragmented or forgotten. It simply conveys the absurdity and incomprehensibility that violence, disaster, and extreme disability entail. Thus, chaotic narrative can present itself as unpredictable and unbalanced, as the product of mental illness. Discussing her early visits to women's domestic abuse shelters, Elaine Lawless begins with a story of a woman whose narrative revealed that she had 'gone over the deep end': she measured the placement of the smallest items in her house to detect if they had been moved by an intruder and left small traps should he show up, convinced that he entered her house on a daily—maybe hourly—basis. Broken-hearted, Lawless shares parts of the story in her own published work, though she decides not to provide the woman's name, exact narrative, or voice. She writes,

> That first hot summer I was just a visitor traveling around, soaking in information, smells, sounds, voices and viscerally responding to what I heard and saw. I nearly vomited as we fled from one particularly horrendous situation when we realized a young girl's mind had simply escaped into the safety of madness as she tried to tell us how her stalker had over and over managed to push his way into her house, her bedroom, her body, defying the police, orders of protection, bolt locks on the door, alarm systems, until her brain was mush. Vic and I sat in the 107 degree heat on a concrete curb in a small town in Southern Missouri and wept together after hearing her story, then tried to leave to our own better worlds, only to find we were locked out of our steaming car and had to suffer there for four more hours, unable to go back into the shelter, for what we feared inside was more dangerous than the heat we had to endure on the outside.
>
> (2001, 4)

Writing about the academic publication of narratives of domestic violence, Ann Ferrell notes, "Because traumatic narratives are often disjointed, the presentation of such narratives, without contextualization, opens the possibility that the narrators will be perceived as confused, inarticulate, or unbalanced" (2009, 383). Cathy Winkler was exceedingly conscious of the potential that others would interpret her as insane on the basis of her own chaotic narrative. She writes:

> When the rapist had his body plastered on mine the first time and had begun his battering of my genitals, I began to step outside of myself. My self was pulling away from my body. My essence wanted to get away from the body of mine that the rapist was torturing. Confused, I pulled myself back into my physical body. . . . When I initially wrote the police report, and a year later when I wrote the chapter on the rape attack for the district attorney, I did not mention this. I felt that disassociation was a sign of insanity, and I did not want the police or lawyers to consider me as anything but a "good victim." (Winkler and Hanke 1995, 173)

Because this narrator was painfully aware of the social and legal repercussions of disassociation, she crafted a narrative that adhered less to felt experience and more to perceived norms of coherence.

Often later, when chaotic narratives—or at least parts of them— become tellable, the narrators themselves reflect on their own sanity in the face of the incomprehensible. One of Lawless's narrators, a hospital maintenance worker named Sherri, said:

> I had this belief because I was with Dale at the time—and at home you could look around and there was always—I could clean up after a fight, but there was always a speck of blood somewhere on my walls and I hated that. I hated that. And I had to clean the morgue that was part of my area. Well there was an autopsy table with all the blood. And I had the belief that if I could get all the blood off of that autopsy table that the abuse in my home would stop. I don't know how I associated that. But the morgue was brick, painted brick, you know, it's got those little holes. I would go through with a toothbrush and a toothpick, a wooden toothpick, trying to get the blood out of the holes. Now when I look back at it, it was crazy, but the whole time I was working in the morgue, cleaning the blood, it was somebody else's blood I was cleaning, it wasn't mine. So that was a comfort.
>
> (2001, 171)

The Devaluing of Fact and the Protective Cover of Ambiguity

The idea that a narrative becomes untellable because language disintegrates in the face of trauma or because memory sometimes fails protectively is only part of the narrative chaos pattern. Another element is a continually reported devaluing of fact, accuracy, evidence, and chronology by the narrator—a natural response on the part of one who wishes not to know, not to remember, and not to relive. Nordstrom and Robben note,

> Any rendition of the contradictory realities of violence imposes order and reason on what has been experienced as chaotic. Inasmuch as violence is resolved in narrative the violent event seems also to lose its particularity—i.e., its facthood—once it is written. Together with its facthood, it loses its absurdity and incomprehensibility, paradoxically the very qualities we would like to convey. (1995, 12)

This is the most sensitive part of the chaotic narrative picture, in that it can be seen to support those who would challenge the truth claims of victim/survivors. This devaluing of fact is exactly counter to the needs of the courts and those who wish to see perpetrators of violence prosecuted—including the victims themselves, who want to establish facts but also don't (and can't). But the real paradox is actually in narrative itself, which seeks to infuse the violent event with coherence and comprehensibility. Hirsh writes,

> I understood in retrospect that establishing the story of what really happened was perhaps what victims (including me) most craved and most feared, and why my notes and reflections would avoid it. . . . If all the pieces of the story about the bombings *were* put together, they would depict the loss, the void, the inchoate underlying the experience, a confirmation yet again of absence, of an old self and cherished others. (2007, 158; italics in original)

Similarly, Winkler argues that purposeful ambiguity protects the victim/survivor:

> In rape attacks, victim survivors suffer ambiguity to intentionally protect themselves from the intensity of the torture or as a result of the impact of the rape trauma. Legal experts want victim survivors to be absolutely accurate yet fail to understand that lack of accuracy is proof that a rape has occurred. Ambiguity exists and is evidence, evidence of a rape attack. (1995, 176)

Speaking For, About, or Without

Despite trauma survivors' sometimes necessary protective recourse to incomprehensibility, ambiguity, and absurdity, coherence, conciseness, and cohesion remain a crucial part of our cultural aesthetic for narrative. It is paradoxical that, at a time when fragmentation is prominent and valorized in postmodern writing, we still preserve—and even strive for—coherence and continuity in representational voices, assuming imbalance and mental illness where coherence is lacking (Rimmon-Kenan 2002, 19). Peter Brooks, a psychoanalytically oriented literary theorist, goes so far as to define mental illness on the basis of narrative coherence. He argues, "[M]ental health is a coherent life story, neurosis is faulty narrative" (1994, 49). Brooks is not alone. Numerous articles about narrative incoherence as an indicator of schizophrenia, manic-depression, and delusional thinking have been published in mental health journals (see, for example, Lysaker 2002). In general, it appears that many people—scholars and laypeople alike—associate a chaotic narrative with a chaotic mind, incoherence with insanity.

As folklorists, we treat narrative as if it provides access to the perspectives and experiences of individuals who lack the power to make their voices heard through other modes of academic and political discourse. The unfortunate result, however, is quite often the inclusion of voices that need to be heard, but that are destabilized, chaotic, desperate, and incoherent, and that therefore reinforce every stereotype we loathe of the traumatized person: the unbalanced, abused housewife; the oversexed rape victim; the crazy war vet. These are not minor issues: the legal repercussions of chaotic narratives can be huge for the victim of a rape hoping to prove her rapist guilty, for the abused wife hoping to incarcerate or at least create distance from her brutal husband, for the refugee looking for sanctuary, for the survivor of a disaster looking for emergency relief, and for the intellectually challenged individual who doesn't want to appear crazy. Is the chaotic voice really able to be heard in a culture that reveres coherence and continuity? And what does our fear of ventriloquism do to the already traumatized, already stigmatized, chaotic narrator?

My argument is not intended to minimize the import of presentation and representation in those arenas involving traumatic experience, violence, and horror; and it is certainly not an argument for silence.[6] Indeed, I contend that the chaotic voice *must* be heard. I believe that it is our responsibility to write in the face of injustice, remembering always that representation and power are intertwined, and that violence, trauma, and mental illness have been largely neglected in the ethnographic literature until quite recently. In fact,

Laura McClusky writes that although anthropologists "have regularly dealt with unsavoury subjects: cannibalism, infanticide, ritual warfare, suttee, genital mutilation, the spread of AIDS, foot binding, colonialization, witchcraft, and genocide, to name a few, domestic violence appears to be a topic that is 'too ugly' to write about" (2001, 7). And Philippe Bourgois commented that he was reluctant to write about rape in his study of crack dealers in the Barrio, because "few people talk about rape—neither the perpetrators nor the victims. In fact, rape is so taboo that I was tempted to omit this discussion" (1995, 207). Lack of ethnographic representation simply adds to the stigma and, thus, to the untellability.

But we also have to be cautious about representation that perpetuates negative stereotypes about victims/survivors, and equally as cautious about the sensationalizing that can easily result from the choices we make about which chaotic narratives to include in our publications. At the same time as we attempt to ensure that the voices of stigmatized individuals are represented, we must also take care, as Shuman and Bohmer (this volume) remind us, not to enter the chaotic narrative into "discourses of veneration." In other words, we should not sacrifice the integrity of narrators and their experiences to our desire for a powerful story that indexes the extent of trauma or disability. The lure of chaos can be tempting in its powerful actuality, in the way it renders trauma and violence experiential and real.[7]

I would argue that sometimes speaking for, about, or without is the better choice. This is not to say that the stories of those who are traumatized should be stricken from our writings, nor am I arguing that trauma stories should never be quoted. Traumatic narratives and chaotic narratives are not one and the same, and time often converts one into the other. But I think it is our job to know the difference—to think about reader response, and to think with and sometimes for those whose stories we represent. Chaos requires care. I agree with Lawless when she writes,

> I am convinced, now, that we must hear and "read" these stories as they come to us, even interrupted and broken by the gaps and ruptures. In fact to ask trauma survivors to go back and fill in the gaps may be to ask them something they are not ready or able to do. Respecting the gaps and ruptures and learning how to peer through them where they bleed into the narrative event but away from recognized language is, rather, our task. (2001, 58)

Proper contextualization can help, as Ferrell notes (2009), but the problem I ran into with Ray Mercer's statements was that no matter how much context I provided, the impact of his words held sway, actualizing, distracting, and representing with the power of presence. That is both the very reason we fill our work with the voices of those we represent and also the reason chaotic narratives threaten to misrepresent.

> Unfortunately, by conceptualizing the narrator of chaotic stories as a subject who lacks the power of self-representation, we can end up regressively reinforcing the power relations that Other the speaker/survivor. Trinh T. Minh-ha explains the grounds for skepticism about whether it is ever possible to adequately or justifiably speak for others by writing that anthropology is mainly a conversation of "us" with "us" about "them," of the white man with the white man about the primitive-nature man . . . in which "them" is silenced. "Them" always stands on the other side of the hill, naked and speechless. . . . "[T]hem" is only admitted among "us," the discussing subjects, when accompanied or introduced by "us."
>
> (1989, 65, 67)

Spivak (1988) argues that only by altering the power relations that construct the subaltern can the subaltern speak in a way that carries the authority to alter the relations of subalternity. For that reason, in chaotic narration situations, narrator re-appropriation of control and voice is perhaps the best alternative, allowing the narrator to reassert personal power.

Cathy Winkler (1995) masterfully takes her chaotic narrative and re-interprets it for her audience. Taking back the control, she writes,

> When I have previously written articles about horrors such as those presented here, most readers do not give me any response. This is probably because they do not know what to say. Therefore I have provided . . . a number of possible responses: the first group includes comments to be avoided; the second group includes comments I . . . and other[s] would appreciate.

Unacceptable responses:

- Great article on your rape
- I loved reading about how horrifying it was
- Now I know what rape is
- How did you get that information

Preferred responses:

- This is a heroic piece of writing
- Your writing is insightful, clear and appreciated
- Thank you for having the courage to educate us
- We all need to learn to take risks like you have, and I am willing to speak up

Best response:

- This is great, fantastic, outstanding. You must be equally great, fantastic, outstanding.

(80)

By re-appropriating her narrative, Winkler regains discursive power. Of course, Winkler's unique position as her own ethnographer allows her to achieve a level of representative control not afforded to most chaotic narrators.

So, not being Winkler, what solutions are left to the author who faces the difficult publication of others' chaotic narratives? The representational problem of speaking for others is based in the notion that a speaker's social location and positionality have a significant impact on how speech is received. Steeped in the lessons of ethnography of speaking, discourse analysis, and genre and performance studies, we know that who says something can drastically affect how it gets heard. Perhaps more significantly, the practice of privileged people speaking on behalf of less privileged people can easily result in reinforcing the oppression of those spoken for (Alcoff 1991, 7). So when is speaking for others a legitimate practice? When can we engage in ventriloquism without also engaging simultaneously in discursive imperialism?

Continual evaluation of the positionality, content, and context of our words and those of our informants is crucial. As Alcoff notes, "One cannot simply look at the [social] location of the speaker or her credentials to speak, nor can one look merely at the propositional content of the speech; one must look at where the speech goes and what it does there" (1991, 26). The crucial question Alcoff asks, and the one we should use when speaking for others, is this: will our ventriloquism enhance the empowerment of those whose voices are lost?

I think that it is something of a truism that the stories that most need to be heard are the ones that are least able to be spoken. But

I also believe that quoting chaotic narrative does not necessarily allow the individual to represent his or her self, because the chaos, as we have seen from the experiences discussed above, all too often consumes the self. If our ethical ideals are about allowing individuals to speak for themselves and about ensuring that the people we write about are able to exert a degree of control over their representations, then we also have to recognize that chaotic narratives may not be a fair or true representation, may not empower, and might ultimately do violence to those who have already faced so much.

Notes

1. "Fall for the Book" began in 1999 as a two-day event organized by George Mason University and the City of Fairfax, Virginia. According to the event's website, it has since expanded into a "week-long, multiple-venue" literary festival that incorporates writing workshops, author meet-and-greets, readings, lectures, and other educational initiatives intended to involve diverse audiences in aspects of reading, writing, and publishing (2012).

2. To be honest, I am still not convinced that I would have left out Ray's comments if given the chance to rethink this decision; however, I believe that I would contextualize the comments with greater caution if I could do it again. The fact that I am still unsure of how best to handle this issue is evidence of the complexity of representational politics.

3. McAdams continues, "While coherence, then, may refer to the structure or form of a story, it may also pertain to a story's content. A story that depicts events or happenings that defy the listener's understanding of how the world works and how human beings typically act, think, feel, and want may seem as incoherent as one that violates structural norms" (2006, 112).

4. Of course, this is tied to debates concerning transcription and ethnopoetic analysis, which question the ethnocentric imposed linearity of narrative reflected in transcription style. See for example, the work of Dennis Tedlock (1972,1983) and Dell Hymes (1977, 1981).

5. I am grateful to the journal editors for helping me to articulate this point.

6. Certainly it has been frequently argued that victims/survivors recover through narrating their trauma. For example, Brison argues: "The communicative act of bearing witness to traumatic events not only transforms traumatic memories into narratives that can then be integrated into the survivor's sense of self and view of the world, but it also reintegrates the survivor into a community, reestablishing bonds of trust and faith in others" (2002, xi).

7. Carolyn Nordstrom argues that we abstract violence—that, to use Taussig's term, we "thing-ify" it (1987, 219). Nordstrom writes, "In Western epistemology, we have a legacy of thinking about violence as a concept, a phenomenon, a thing, rather than recognizing it as experiential and rendering it real" (1995, 138).

References

Alcoff, Linda. 1991. "The Problem of Speaking For Others." *Cultural Critique* 20:5–32.

Bletzer, Keith V., and Mary P. Koss. 2004. "Narrative Constructions of Sexual Violence as Told by Female Rape Survivors in Three Populations of the Southwestern United States: Scripts of Coercion, Scripts of Consent." *Medical Anthropology* 23 (2): 113–56.

Booth, Tim, and Wendy Booth. 1996. "Sounds of Silence: Narrative Research with Inarticulate Subjects." *Disability and Society* 11 (1): 55–69.

Bourgois, Philippe. 1995. *In Search of Respect: Selling Crack in El Barrio.* New York: Cambridge University Press.

Brison, Susan J. 2002. *Aftermath: Violence and the Remaking of the Self.* Princeton, NJ: Princeton University Press.

Brooks, Peter. 1994. *Psychoanalysis and Storytelling.* Oxford: Blackwell.

Capps, Lisa, and Elinor Ochs. 1995. "Out of Place: Narrative Insights into Agoraphobia." *Discourse Processes* 19 (3): 407–39.

Clifford, James. 1986. "Introduction: Partial Truths." In *Writing Culture: The Poetics and Politics of Ethnography*, edited by James Clifford and George E. Marcus, 1–26. Berkeley and Los Angeles: University of California Press.

———. 1988. *The Predicament of Culture: Twentieth-Century Ethnography, Literature, and Art.* Cambridge, MA: Harvard University Press.

Culbertson, Roberta. 1995. "Embodied Memory, Transcendence and Telling: Recounting Trauma, Re-establishing the Self." *New Literary History* 26:169–95.

Fall for the Book. 2012. "About Fall for the Book." http://www.fallforthe-book.org/about.php (accessed August 6).

Ferrell, Ann K. 2009. Review of These Are Our Stories: Women's Stories of Abuse and Survival, edited by Jan Rosenberg. *Western Folklore* 68 (2/3): 382–83.

Frank, Arthur W. 1995. *The Wounded Storyteller: Body, Illness and Ethics.* Chicago: University of Chicago Press.

Goldstein, Diane E. 2004. *Once Upon a Virus: Aids Legends and Vernacular Risk Perception.* Logan: Utah State University Press.

———. 2009. "The Sounds of Silence: Foreknowledge, Miracles, Suppressed Narratives and Terrorism—What Not Telling Might Tell Us." *Western Folklore* 68 (3): 235–57.

Heath, Shirley Brice. 1983. *Ways with Words: Language, Life, and Work in Communities and Classrooms.* Cambridge: Cambridge University Press.

Hesford, Wendy S. 1999. "Reading Rape Stories: Material Rhetoric and the Trauma of Representation." *College English* 62 (2): 192–21.

Hirsh, Susan F. 2007. "Writing Ethnography After Tragedy: Toward Therapeutic Transformations," *Political and Legal Anthropological Review* 30 (1): 151–79.

Howell, Jayne. 2004. "Turning Out Good Ethnography, or Talking Out of Turn? Gender, Violence, and Confidentiality in Southeastern Mexico." *Journal of Contemporary Ethnography* 33:323–52.

Huynh Chau Nguyen, Nathalie. 2008. "Memory and Silence in the Vietnamese Diaspora: The Narratives of Two Sisters." *Oral History* 36 (2): 64–74.

Hymes, Dell. 1977. "Discovering Oral Performance and Measured Verse in American Indian Narrative." *New Literary History* 7: 431–57.

———. 1981. "In Vain I Tried to Tell You": *Essays in Native American Ethnopoetics.* Philadelphia: University of Pennsylvania Press.

Labov, William, and Joshua Waletzky. 1967. "Narrative Analysis: Oral Versions of Personal Experience." In *Essays on the Verbal and Visual Arts,* edited by June L. Helm, 12–44. Seattle: University of Washington Press.

Lawless, Elaine J. 2001. *Women Escaping Violence: Empowerment through Narrative.* Columbia: University of Missouri Press.

Lysaker, Paul Henry. 2002. "Narrative Structure in Psychosis Schizophrenia and Disruptions in the Dialogical Self." *Theory and Psychology* 12 (2): 207–20.

McClusky, Laura J. 2001. *Here Our Culture Is Hard: Stories of Domestic Violence from a Mayan Community in Belize.* Austin: University of Texas Press.

McAdams, Dan P. 2006. "The Problem of Narrative Coherence." *Journal of Constructivist Psychology* 19:109–25.

Medved, Maria. 2004. "Making Sense of Traumatic Experiences: Telling Your Life with Fragile X Syndrome." *Qualitative Health Research* 14 (6): 741–59.

Mills, Margaret A. 1991. *Rhetorics and Politics in Afghan Traditional Storytelling.* Philadelphia: University of Pennsylvania Press.

Nordstrom, Carolyn. 1995. "War on the Front Lines." In *Fieldwork under Fire: Contemporary Studies of Violence and Survival,* edited by Carolyn Nordstrom and Antonius C. G. M. Robben, 129–55. Berkeley and Los Angeles: University of California Press.

Nordstrom, Carolyn, and Antonius C. G. M. Robben, eds. 1995. *Fieldwork under Fire: Contemporary Studies of Violence and Survival.* Berkeley and Los Angeles: University of California Press.

Norrick, Neal R. 2005. "The Dark Side of Tellability." *Narrative Inquiry* 15 (2): 323–43.

Ramanathan, Vai. 1995. "Narrative Well-formedness in Alzheimer's Discourse: An Interactional Examination across Settings." *Journal of Pragmatics* 23:395–419.

Rimmon-Kenan, Shlomith. 2002. "The Story of 'I': Illness and Narrative Identity." *Narrative* 10 (1): 9–27.

Ritchie, Susan. 1993. "Ventriloquist Folklore: Who Speaks For Representation?" *Western Folklore* 52 (2): 365–78.

Sacks, Harvey. 1992. *Lectures on Conversation.* Edited by Gail Jefferson. Oxford: Blackwell.

Scarry, Elaine. 1985. *The Body in Pain: The Making and Unmaking of the World.* Oxford: Oxford University Press.

Shuman, Amy. 2006. "Entitlement and Empathy in Personal Narrative." *Narrative Inquiry* 16 (1): 148–55.

Shuman, Amy, and Carol Bohmer. 2004. "Representing Trauma: Political Asylum Narrative." *Journal of American Folklore* 117 (466): 394–414.

Spivak, Gayatri Chakravorty. 1988. "Can the Subaltern Speak?" In *Marxism and the Interpretation of Culture,* edited by Cary Nelson and Lawrence Grossberg, 271–313. Urbana and Chicago: University of Illinois Press.

Taussig, Michael. 1987. *Shamanism, Colonialism, and the Wild Man: A Study in Terror and Healing.* Chicago, IL: University of Chicago Press.

Tedlock, Dennis, trans. 1972. *Finding the Center: Narrative Poetry of the Zuni Indians.* Lincoln: University of Nebraska Press.

——. 1983. *The Spoken Word and the Work of Interpretation.* Philadelphia: University of Pennsylvania Press.

Trinh, Thi Minh-ha. 1989. *Woman, Native, Other: Writing Postcoloniality and Feminism.* Bloomington: Indiana University Press.

Van der Kolk, Bessel A., James Hopper, and Janet E. Osterman. 2001. "Exploring the Nature of Traumatic Memory: Combining Clinical Knowledge with Laboratory Methods." *Journal of Aggression, Maltreatment, and Trauma* 4 (1): 9–32.

Winkler, Cathy, and Penelope Hanke. 1995. "Ethnography of the Ethnographer." In *Fieldwork Under Fire: Contemporary Studies of Violence and Survival,* edited by Carolyn Nordstrom and Antonius C. G. M. Robben, 155–85. Berkeley and Los Angeles: University of California Press.

Wycoff, Donna. 1996. "Now Everything Makes Sense: Complicating the Contemporary Legend Picture." In *Contemporary Legend: A Reader,* edited by Gillian Bennett and Paul Smith, 363–80. New York: Garland.

DIANE E. GOLDSTEIN is Professor and former Chair of the Department of Folklore and Ethnomusicology at Indiana University and is the former President of the American Folklore Society, 2012–2013. Her publications include *Talking AIDS: Interdisciplinary Perspectives on Acquired Immune Deficiency Syndrome, Once Upon a Virus: AIDS Legends and Vernacular Risk Perception* and *Haunting Experiences: Ghosts in Contemporary Folklore.*

4   The Stigmatized Vernacular: Political Asylum and the Politics of Visibility/ Recognition

STIGMA IS A fundamental concept for folkloristics, first as a dimension of 'the folk' as other, subaltern, or minority—a status not always accompanied by stigma—and second as a dimension of how those groups manage their identities and negotiate recognition. Folklorists have a long history of wrestling with the complexities of sympathetic representations of stigmatized groups. Folklorists have an implicit mandate to avoid ethnocentric judgment, a long heritage of championing social justice, and a history of ongoing dialogue about what to do when placed in the uncomfortable position of describing politically or socially less acceptable cultural practices. Sometimes, folklorists have been in the position of collaborating with members of a group in order to recuperate or identify the group's positive value, whether as explicit advocates or as crafters of sympathetic representations.

Study of the stigmatized vernacular—that is, attending to how particular practices of everyday life are marked and repudiated—contributes to existing related discussions, including those that treat ethnocentrism, cultural relativism, discrimination, stereotyping, and identity politics. We suggest that the concept of the stigmatized vernacular additionally calls attention to how stigma relies upon the stability of what counts as normal. In this essay, we explore how stigma and normalcy produce each other; in addition, we consider the experiences of individuals whose normal, ordinary, familiar worlds have radically changed or disappeared as a result of political violence. Folklorists are familiar with the fact that cultural conventions regarding what is ordinary and familiar always change. We add to that discussion by considering the disappearance of the ordinary, or more precisely, the experience of routinized violence as a different kind of ordinary for people who then seek asylum in a new country. We observe how immigration officials in political asylum hearings sometimes further stigmatize victims of persecution by insisting on their own categories of 'normal.' After a general discussion of the stigmatized vernacular and folklore, we will turn to an in-depth account of political asylum and stigma, represented through a description of a Cameroonian woman's asylum case.

Initially, we approached the study of political asylum with the observation that in some cases, immigration officials' rejections of applicants revealed a lack of understanding of cultural context. However, after reviewing dozens of cases of what looked like absurd denials, we decided to pay more attention to what we came to call the 'lens of suspicion' through which asylum officers typically evaluate cases. We propose that attention to the cultural context of the asylum applicants is insufficient for determining the legitimacy of their claims. More generally, any assessment of cultural context that depends on cultural norms is insufficient for understanding stigmatizing situations. Conceptualizing 'the normal' is itself a means for enacting exclusions. In the case of political asylum hearings, if a cultural practice or situation is not recognized as falling within what the officials are willing to accept as plausible, the application will fail. In our work with asylum seekers, we have documented several cases in which culturally specific experiences of violence and persecution did not conform to the officials' expectations and presumptions. At the same time, we recognize that taking cultural context into account is insufficient for understanding how norms are imposed and sustained. Violence can become routinized, creating regimes of exclusion that appear to be 'normal.' For example, asylum officials have denied applications by lesbians requesting political asylum, arguing that they should return to their home countries and act "discreetly" in order to avoid persecution. The stigmatized vernacular can be a pervasive mechanism for concealing discrimination under the guise of what is 'normal.'

In this essay we discuss stigmatizing practices in the context of a politics of visibility and tellability: we consider how stigma can render groups visible/invisible/hypervisible and can render their stories untellable. In other words, stigma is part of larger processes of recognition, misrecognition, estrangement, and othering. Our research focuses on political asylum applicants who have experienced stigma, discrimination, and persecution in their home countries and who often face further stigma when their political asylum claims are labeled fraudulent by asylum officials. In many cases, applicants for political asylum not only have been disqualified for normal, ordinary categories of social life in their home countries, but the extreme consequences of stigma as discrimination and persecution have also destroyed whatever was once familiar to them.

Finally, we suggest some disciplinary applications. Conceptualizing the stigmatized vernacular involves describing how what might otherwise be normal or ordinary situations and experiences become defamiliarized, estranged, marked as other. For folklorists, the study of the stigmatized vernacular is part of a tension between the repudiated and the celebrated. Carol Silverman's (2012) study of Romani music and culture begins by observing that many groups revere Romani music but discriminate against Romani people. The repudiated and the venerated rarely exist in isolation; rather, they are connected to each other through processes of valuation, devaluation, and revaluation. For folklorists, the stigmatized vernacular is part of the relations between forms and values that characterize all cultural practices: all forms of expressive culture—whether they be genres, material productions, or performances—always have value.

Thus folklorists, who recognize stigma as an unfortunately pervasive dimension of inter-group relations, have much to add to conversations about human rights, cultural relativism, normalcy, and abnormalcy. A folkloric approach to stigma would 1) attend to how stigma is associated with particular cultural constructions of normalcy by using ethnography to document what is considered normal/abnormal, by whom, about whom, and in which contexts; 2) observe the performative, interactional facets of stigma ('passing,' associating with fellow travelers, etc.) as both a dimension of social group networks and as a dimension of performance in everyday life; 3) provide a close analysis of both discourses and interactions to identify how stigma is enacted through different genres, including jokes, narratives, folk drama, etc.; 4) observe cultural expectations of the tellability and untellability of those genres in different contexts; and 5) attend to how stigmatized groups position themselves with regard to whatever is considered normal or ordinary as a part of belonging to a particular folk group.

Normalcy, the Ordinary, and Cultural Relativism

One of the most valuable contributions of Erving Goffman's understanding of stigma was his observation that discrimination on the basis of perceived difference (physical, racial, cultural, etc.) excludes individuals from participation in whatever is considered normal (1963, 2). That is, stigma and normalcy produce each other: stigmatization places a group outside the bounds of what is considered ordinary, acceptable, and expected by others; members of stigmatized groups are deprived of (Goffman says "disqualified" from) being normal. As Goffman points out, individuals sometimes take on the stigmas assigned to them by others. But many stigmatized individuals determine to be ordinary on their own terms, that is, without changing to conform to others' categories of what counts as normal. Further, when something otherwise ordinary is denied, it loses its status as given and can become instead a site of discrimination. The plea for redress can be an appeal for a restoration of the ordinary. For example, in his 2009 plenary address to the American Folklore Society—an account of how folklorists celebrate the ordinary—Roger Welsch told a story about arranging for a Native American group to bury the remains of their desecrated ancestors on his property. What the Native American group wanted was something very ordinary: burying their ancestors properly.

Most of the research on stigma following Goffman has focused on how people manage their "spoiled identities" (Goffman 1963) and on the consequences of stereotyping for self-esteem or social status, rather than on stigmatizing processes in cultural interaction. What is neglected in the majority of research on stigma is attention to what Goffman describes as "the normals" (1963, 5) or what Lennard Davis (1995, 2006) has described as normalcy,[1] and the ways that stigma and normalcy produce each other. Davis, a leading disabilities scholar, calls attention to normalcy as an ideological construct. As in anthropological discussions of cultural relativism (Herskovits 1972), the critique of normalcy articulates a position of estrangement, a heightened awareness of the constructedness of the taken-for-granted world, and especially of the judgments implicit in identifying some experiences as 'normal.'[2] As Alison Dundes Renteln points out, cultural relativism is "not just the recognition of cultural differences in thought, value, and action. It is a theory about the way in which evaluations or judgments are made" (1988, 57). Renteln specifically links the concept of cultural relativism to normalcy, referring in particular to Ruth Benedict's observations that normal and abnormal are culturally specific categories (58).

The concept of the stigmatized vernacular thus provides an opportunity to move beyond old arguments about the inadequacies of the concept of cultural relativism, especially with regard to the possible contradiction between cultural relativism and human rights (Dembour 1996; Khanna 2006). Renteln argues that this is not a necessary contradiction because relativism does not imply tolerance (1988, 68). As we will discuss, the political asylum process, a human rights endeavor, is a useful example of the problem that recognizing cultural difference does not inevitably lead to greater tolerance. In the example of the political asylum process we discuss here, more often asylum seekers are stigmatized for cultural differences that do not fit the mold of expectations for asylum.

Stigma, Estrangement, and Political Asylum

The authors have been working with political asylum applicants for more than a decade. Beginning in the 1990s Carol Bohmer, a sociologist and lawyer, volunteered her services at Community Refugee Immigration Services in Columbus, Ohio, and she has continued her work in New England and the United Kingdom. Amy Shuman, a folklorist, initially collaborated with Bohmer to identify problems of narrative faced by the asylum seekers. After co-publishing work on narrative and asylum (Bohmer and Shuman 2004), we wrote a book designed to provide a comprehensive discussion of the problems asylum seekers experience with the immigration systems in the United States and the United Kingdom. That book, *Rejecting Refugees* (Bohmer and Shuman 2008), was informed by both ethnographic and legal perspectives, but it was written without academic jargon: our intended audience was asylum seekers and those who assist them. Here, as in all of our publications, we have drawn upon already published cases (whether in print or online) rather than describe the individuals with whom we have worked. We are wary of subjecting these individuals or their families and associates to any jeopardy, and we are aware of how easily someone can be traced through us, even if we use pseudonyms and change places of origin. In some cases we have perceived more risk than our interlocutors did; for example, Margaretta, whose case we discuss here, requested that we write about her story.[3]

Political asylum applicants are multiply stigmatized in the immigration process. As we discuss at greater length in *Rejecting Refugees*, applicants from some countries are treated more favorably than others. Mothers can be stigmatized for leaving their children behind; applicants who enter the United States or United Kingdom with false documents or without documents are considered criminals. The applicants, having suffered catastrophic and violent loss of their everyday lives and cultural traditions, understandably describe out-of the-ordinary circumstances but face the task of convincing the officials that their stories are credible (Bloomaert 2001; Einhorn 2009; Jacquemet 1996; Ranger 2008; Schuster 2003). Lacking many of the markers of credibility, such as proof of identity or documentation of what they suffered, these individuals rely on their narratives to prove that they are who they say they are and that the things they describe really happened (Bohmer and Shuman 2008). As Goffman noted, the stigmatized are discredited; this certainly applies to the asylum seeker, though the result of being discredited has the extreme consequence of deportation.

Goffman conceptualizes stigma as a process of estrangement in which individuals discover that they are disqualified for whatever counts as normal (1963, 80). The concept of estrangement—making the familiar strange—is fundamental to ethnography and has its roots in the politics of oppression, from the Russian Formalists' concept of estrangement in the novel (Herzfeld 2005) to Paulo Freire's argument (1974) that resisting oppression requires a process of externalization through which people who have been the objects of symbolic and physical violence begin by naming and reading the world.

Estrangement works in multiple directions. As in the case of stigma or stereotype, it can be a process of othering others as different and then differently valued, or a process of self-recognition of that othering, or alienation from a dominant ideological formation. In the narratives we discuss here, Margaretta, a Cameroonian political asylum applicant in the United States, describes how she was stigmatized in Cameroon because she spoke English, discrimination that resulted in her being deprived of her nursing certificate. She protested along with other students, was imprisoned, raped, and then faced further imprisonment in a prison from which, she said, no one ever left. She was able to escape, travel to the United States and apply for political asylum. Twice, her asylum application was denied: as is common in the political asylum application process, her case was considered insufficient, in large part because her story was not deemed credible. We will argue that the asylum seekers and the asylum officials operate with different vernaculars, different conceptions of what counts as normal, and that in the context of the political asylum hearing, that difference renders the asylum seekers' experiences untellable and renders them unrecognizable.[4] Of course, some applicants are successful, but we suggest that in both cases—those accepted and those denied—asylum seekers are subject to an asylum official's assumptions about what is credible.

For the past ten years, we have been collecting narratives from people applying for political asylum in the United States and United Kingdom.[5] These are people fleeing persecution more horrendous than stigma or discrimination—but as part of their experiences, they describe being made into outcasts. They describe not only the pain of stigmatization, but also their longing for an ordinary life that has been destroyed and that will not be recovered. The success of their applications depends on persuading immigration officials that they have a "well-founded fear" of returning home. In order to do this, they have to reconstruct life as they knew it and life as it became in conditions of persecution; they must also communicate the impossibility of returning to a home that in many cases no longer exists. The task of the immigration official is to determine whether or not return is possible: according to the international law of non-refoulement, people cannot be returned to a home country where they would face persecution or danger.[6] The asylum official thus needs to determine whether the applicant's story is credible and whether the home country is safe for that person. Both determinations depend on assessments of what is credible/normal/possible.

Asylum officials determine credibility based on several factors, including the applicant's demeanor, whether or not the description of the persecution conforms to what the official knows about the situation in the applicant's home country, whether there are any inconsistencies in the application, whether the official has heard similar accounts and therefore considers the applicant's account to be a stock story, and whether the applicant has knowledge that the official would expect him or her to have about the home country, religion, or situation. For example, a female applicant claiming persecution on the grounds of maintaining a sexual relationship with another woman was asked about her knowledge of lesbian bars and magazines (Lewis 2012). The link between the credible and the normal is one of the fault lines in the system. Each measure of credibility depends on the officials' expectations, prior knowledge, and assumptions. The category of the plausible is an extension of the category of the normal. However, an account of atrocities is never normal and therefore always somewhat incredible.

In *Rejecting Refugees*, we review each of these dimensions of credibility; here, we provide a discussion of one case at length in order to explore the complexities of the political asylum review process. Margaretta's credibility was challenged on two grounds: first, the officials doubted that she had escaped from prison through bribery; second, they were suspicious of what they regarded as discrepancies in her account. When she was in prison, she bribed a guard she recognized from her community. The immigration officials were suspicious that a guard would jeopardize his own security and position by accepting a bribe. However, we heard several similar cases in which someone used bribery to escape or to acquire a passport (Bohmer and Shuman 2008). Cameroon was singled out as the most corrupt country in the world in 1999 (Terretta 2012), but the officials still regarded Margaretta's story with suspicion—despite the fact that official 'country reports' also specifically describe corruption. In many asylum cases, we have observed that stories about bribery and other forms of corruption arouse suspicion for the officials (Bohmer and Shuman 2008, 92). Bribery and other forms of corruption are in fact so common that this suspicion is itself strange; below we will return to this problem and consider the relationship between suspicion and tellability in the political asylum process.

Immigration officials use varied means to assess an individual's application. Relying on official 'country reports,' they consider the likelihood of particular kinds of violence occurring in particular places (Bohmer and Shuman 2008; Ramji-Nogales 2009). Cameroon is a relatively stable African country and has good relations with the United States, so many Southern Cameroonian (English-speaking) applicants have faced difficulty gaining asylum. Using Goffman's terminology, we might say that the Cameroonian asylum applicants were potentially "disqualified," that is, stigmatized as potentially fraudulent, from the start. As Meredith Terretta, who served as an expert witness for Cameroonian cases, explains, Cameroonian asylum seekers have often been presumed to be economic migrants (and therefore fraudulent asylum seekers). Terretta argues that US asylum officials regard bribery and the rampant sale of false documents in Cameroon as an economic, rather than a political, problem. As an expert witness, Terretta attempted to correct the officials' assumptions. For example, she explained that a non-governmental building might serve as a prison (2012). Cameroonians were disqualified as asylum seekers because they were placed in a different (that is, economic) category, and they were stigmatized as fraudulent for making asylum claims at all.

Through dozens of examples, Goffman described the experience of exclusion and disqualification resulting from stigma. Goffman's examples identify individuals who are excluded from public participation because of a physical disability or sexual identity (1963, 81). Political asylum seekers have experienced a violent form of stigma: discrimination that turned into persecution. Like any stigmatized group, political asylum seekers are disqualified from a category (*citizen*) that they and others perceive to be normal—and they are disqualified altogether from citizenship, not just from a particular aspect of it. As a Southern Cameroonian nursing student, Margaretta initially was disqualified only from receiving her degree. Later, when she protested, she was disqualified as a citizen. Goffman explains the response to stigma in part as a choice between disclosing the stigma (becoming visible) and concealing the stigma by means of 'passing' or remaining invisible. Many illegal immigrants, including political asylum applicants who have been refused asylum, choose invisibility. Political asylum is part of a politics of invisibility that is one way of managing the situation of being disqualified for citizenship. Drawing on Giorgio Agamben's work (1998), Luca Miggiano argues:

> In such a situation [being denied], the migrant usually chooses to live as irregular in the country. In some sense she is accepted by the state just as *homo sacer*. She is similar to the Agambian encamped, yet different, since she is allowed to live as long as she remains "invisible." This is a relevant difference for our argument. She is, in fact, inside a border but still outside the boundary of citizenship. (2009, 12)

As Miggiano points out, political asylum applicants differ from migrants who live under the radar illegally. Political asylum applicants are within the system but live provisionally, temporarily, awaiting a decision on their application. They have seen the destruction of their ordinary lives, but their status as applicants prevents them from resuming ordinary life. Most specifically, in the United States they cannot work during the first six months of their application process; in the United Kingdom they receive some benefits but cannot work until after they receive asylum.

As mentioned earlier, Margaretta was getting a degree at Buea University in Anglophone Cameroon when the Cameroonian government declared that degrees issued by her program were invalid and that she had to study in French. She and other students protested; she was detained several times and finally was going to be placed in a prison from which, as she said, no one ever left alive. After being raped in prison, she bribed a guard and escaped. She had been accepted for a Fulbright position in the United States, so she was able to go to the US embassy, retrieve her documentation, and come to the United States, where she applied for political asylum. When she left Cameroon and the authorities couldn't find her, they detained, tortured, and killed her brother. Margaretta's application was turned down twice on the grounds of inconsistencies in her story, but with the help of Carol Bohmer and another lawyer, she now has asylum. She can't return to Cameroon, and she says she stays alive only to avoid causing her mother more suffering.

Margaretta's story is not only about being multiply stigmatized as an Anglophone Cameroonian, as a protester, as a raped woman, and, in the United States, as a possible illegal alien rather than a heroic, venerated political prisoner. Her story is also about how catastrophe and violence have deprived her of being an ordinary person doing ordinary things like being a student, a daughter, and a citizen.

"We Can't Be Ourselves Anymore"

As the ground against which stigma is defined, the normal is often taken to be self-evident. To some extent, this is the case in the political asylum process, especially in assumptions that both asylum officials and asylum applicants make about presumed shared knowledge. However, 'normal' is far more often a negotiated category in the political asylum process. First, people fleeing persecution have experienced the loss of whatever was everyday normal life, and the political asylum process requires that they both reconstruct it and demonstrate the impossibility of returning to it.[7] The loss of ordinary life—for example, the means of earning a living—is not sufficient for an asylum claim, but it is part of the narrative. Second, the question of whether or not the persecution someone experienced merits asylum depends on an unstated and unexamined sense of what counts as 'normal' hardship as distinguished from atrocity (see Jackson 2002). Political asylum applicants often describe humiliations, violence, and violation that the officials do not consider serious enough to warrant asylum. Third, asylum officials evaluate the situations in each country differently. What might be normal in one place is considered atrocious in another. As part of the process of assessing political asylum applications to determine whether they are legitimate or fraudulent and whether or not they meet the requirements for asylum, immigration officials rely on country reports that describe the political conditions in a particular country or region. Political asylum law requires that applicants prove a "well-founded fear" that would prevent return to their home countries. Applicants face many hurdles when attempting to prove well-founded fear (Bohmer and Shuman 2008), but often the greatest challenge is created by the officials' assumptions about what is normal and what is extraordinary.

Margaretta's case for political asylum depended on her account of discrimination against English-speaking Cameroonians in general, a situation not well known in 2009, though it was documented at the time on websites.[8] The officials might have accepted her account of being stigmatized as an English-speaking Cameroonian, but stigma is not a sufficient condition for political asylum. Margaretta described the discovery that her nursing degree would not be accredited following the unification of French and Anglophone Cameroon:

> So growing up as a child, I already knew that I was disadvantaged in a way. Because before they created the only English-speaking university, we had to go the French-speaking part of Cameroon for college and graduate study, and we had to study in French. So think about it. You study all your life in English. For elementary school to high school. And suddenly you're studying in French. When we went for our examinations, the French-speaking Cameroonians were laughing at us Anglophones. They were really making fun of us.

In this part of her narrative, told informally to Amy Shuman and not as part of her official political asylum narrative, Margaretta is describing being stigmatized as an English speaker. Stigma escalated to discrimination when the Francophone administrators discredited the nursing program in which Margaretta was enrolled. She describes learning about this:[9]

> When we got the information, and uh one of the professors . . . from the X tribe. We were in the ICU, and he came in. He said, "Oh sorry, you guys have just wasted your time. Your program is no longer accredited." . . . Irrespective of what you know. All that knowledge. Too bad. And so we were like, "Uh oh, something is not right here." So we spoke to some of our faculty members. And the faculty encouraged us. . . . So we organized a demonstration. We went on strike. We didn't go to class. . . . The whole university was very supportive. It just went to validate the fact that we can't be ourselves anymore.

Margaretta's last comment is important. The Anglophone Cameroonians could no longer be themselves. They no longer had the life of ordinary students but instead joined the Southern Cameroon National Council as activists. Margaretta noted, "So I decided to join the organization because I realized that I really had to do something. It wasn't going to get better. I needed to do something. So I joined and I started getting involved."

It was in her role as an activist, while demonstrating against the Anglophone administrative decision, that Margaretta was arrested. As a condition of her release, she was forced to sign a paper saying that she would not participate in future resistance efforts. She continued her activism; after her third arrest, she was going to be sent to a maximum-security prison. In her capacity as a nurse, before her life as an activist, she had rescued someone from that prison, and she knew that few prisoners left alive. She bribed a guard and was able to escape before being sent to the prison. The rationale for denying her asylum case was that she had not sufficiently demonstrated either her membership in the resistance group or her grounds for fearing return. Further, asylum officials asserted that a prison guard would be unlikely to jeopardize his own safety by helping her to escape. Many asylum seekers are denied with similar rationales (Bohmer and Shuman 2010). In our research on political asylum, we have argued that asylum officials need to expand their concept of what is normal or at least understand that normal is always contingent on cultural, historical, and political factors. They need to recognize that in some situations, bribery is normal; in some situations, brothers are killed when their sisters can't be found.[10]

Stigma, Bribery, and the Realignment of Associations

In his 1963 book *Stigma*, Goffman details the variety of possible associations people create in response to stigma. His discussion begins with the stigmatized individual who does not necessarily know, but might seek out, others who are similarly stigmatized. Still focusing on the individual, he provides examples of "the normals," people who find that their status is compromised by their association with stigmatized individuals. Many asylum seekers attempt to describe the persecution they experienced as a result of their association with stigmatized others. Although persecution and discrimination are entirely different in scale, Goffman's framework is useful for understanding the fundamental role that association plays in stigma, discrimination, and persecution.

Margaretta's story is in essence a story about realigned associations. As we noted, she contextualizes her personal account within the larger history of discrimination against Anglophone Cameroonians. When faced with the discreditation of her degree, she first joined with other protesting students and then joined the larger resistance movement. But her associations are not only with "fellow travelers" (to use Goffman's term, 1963, 85, 112–14). Not all of her associations were designed to find shared understanding. One of her most important associations—one that led to her arrangement with the prison guard— was grounded in her social world apart from her life as a student and activist. She was acquainted with the guard through two connections: in her role as a nurse, she had treated his wife; she also knew one of his relatives. Before the discrimination against Anglophone nursing students, and before they protested this discrimination, Margaretta and the guard were affiliated in the medical domain. In the political domain, they were reconfigured as prisoner and guard, as enemies on different sides of a political struggle. Margaretta strategically called upon their earlier relationship when negotiating a means for her escape.

Political asylum officials are often suspicious of complex associations such as these, even though many applicants describe associations that Margaretta also experienced. She joined the resistance group not because of a longstanding ideological conviction, but rather because she felt compelled to act when faced with discrimination. In her search for help, she relied not only on people who shared her stigma and her experiences, but also on those one might call her enemies. Although the asylum officials seem to regard bribery as an association that compromises an asylum applicant's integrity, and thus her credibility (Terretta 2012), bribery can be more accurately understood in this case as part of an already compromised situation. Bribery involves irregular and contradictory associations that rely upon trust as well as power and corruption. Political asylum applicants report a variety of situations requiring bribery; these include, but are not limited to, using bribery to escape detention. People extract bribes for helping migrants and people fleeing persecution to obtain passports, visas, or other documents and for helping them cross borders and arrange transport.

Bribery is endemic to situations of persecution, and yet it is a cause for suspicion among immigration officials, who themselves are sometimes accused of requesting or accepting bribes (*New York Times* 1999). Bribery is an example of strange associations that become, in some situations, normal. Bribery draws on dimensions of the lost former ordinary life in which, for example, a man brings his wife to the doctor, and they become acquainted with a nurse. That ordinary association acquires different, but also ordinary (normal) significance when the man, as prison guard, can be bribed by the nurse, as prisoner. However, the asylum official involved in bribery is not part of a new normal, ordinary, association, but instead represents corruption, something that can threaten the ordinary. The failure of immigration officials to recognize that bribery is normal, rather than a sign of corruption that challenges the integrity of an asylum applicant, is not surprising when understood in terms of the larger context of the failure to recognize how violence becomes ordinary. As in domestic violence, unrecognizable associations (between people who are either supposed to be friends or supposed to be enemies) can render accounts of those associations untellable.

The Stigmatized Vernacular and Untellability

As Goffman observed, people with invisible stigmas often face a choice between disclosing or concealing their situation. Disclosure can invite exclusions and rejections; furthermore, in many cases people who reveal their stigma do not feel recognized or understood. Goffman does not fully address the conditions of recognition, and he limits his discussion to more obvious differences (visible scars, skin color, or disabilities) rather than addressing other conditions that bear on the complexities of invisibility and stigma.

People fleeing atrocity, for instance, are often in the impossible situation of having experienced humiliation and violence that they not only prefer not to recall, but that, in many cases, they cannot speak of. Margaretta was so threatened by the immigration officials in her first two hearings that she did not, and felt that she could not, tell them that she had been raped in prison. As part of the process of assisting Margaretta for her second hearing, Carol Bohmer called her weekly and asked her to tell her story. Carol worried that although these rehearsals were necessary for the success of the case, she was subjecting Margaretta to weekly emotional suffering. However, Margaretta described these sessions to Amy Shuman as "having the feeling of being someone somebody cares about."

Margaretta said, "Carol made a huge difference. A huge difference. She was very helpful. Carol—I can't tell you what she means to me. I can't even tell you. Every week, she made me have the feeling of being someone somebody cares about. She can never understand that."

Much has been written about the role of the witness who listens to trauma narratives (Caruth 1995; Culbertson 1995). In an interview with Cathy Caruth, Robert Lifton says,

> One has had this experience, it has been over-whelming, the self has been shattered in some degree; the only way one can feel right or justified in reconstituting oneself and going on living with some vitality is to carry through one's responsibility to the dead. And it's carrying through that responsibility via one's witness, that survivor mission, that enables one to be an integrated human being once more. (1995, 138)

Both authors of the present article, but Carol Bohmer especially, have served in the role of witness to asylum seekers' trauma narratives. As witnesses, we have helped asylum seekers tell stories that are multiply untellable: sometimes the narratives are about topics that are rarely if ever talked about in the tellers' native cultures; in some cases, the asylum process renders these stories untellable, such as when the translator's tribal or class status inhibits an applicant's full disclosure. The asylum process itself also creates conditions for what is tellable.

One of the immigration officials in *Well-Founded Fear* (Robertson and Camerini 2000) describes the experience of hearing an applicant's story as "humbling," although the more typical relationship is that of interrogator and interrogated, with conversations filtered through a lens of suspicion. Put most simply, suspicion depends and creates categories of what counts as credible, and within that framework, narratives that do not fit the mold of the acceptable, expected script are not tellable. In Nancy Campbell's terms, "Technologies of suspicion are predicated upon a framework of trust; they are deployed within a 'system of takings-for-granted' that presupposes trust and thus makes distrust possible" (2004, 78).

Goffman discusses the problem of the tellable within the larger contexts of public life and visibility. He points out that people conceal stigma to pass as 'normal,' and disclosure has a variety of motivations—for example, those who reveal stigma may desire to connect with someone who shares the stigma or to resist an imposed silence. For political asylum applicants (as for many others in Goffman's examples), *passing* means to be recognized as legitimate. The criteria are not only the interactional measures of whether someone has successfully convinced others that they are who they say they are, although this is a crucial factor (Bohmer and Shuman 2007). In addition, for political asylum seekers, there are legal criteria that make a person unrecognizable to the state (Veena Das describes this condition as being "illegible" [2007, 162]). Being able to speak, as difficult as that may be, is not sufficient for providing recognition.

Becoming Illegible and Unrecognizable: The Loss of the Ordinary

The ordinary and the normal are two of the conditions for recognition, and the loss of the ordinary—especially the violent and catastrophic interruption of any possibility of ordinary life—often makes people unrecognizable, underlining and intensifying the hegemony of normalcy. In *Rejecting Refugees* (Bohmer and Shuman 2008) we wrote mostly about the process of applying for political asylum, but the stories the asylum seekers told us were as much about their experience of loss of family and ordinary life as they were about the catastrophes they experienced. Part of the problem that Margaretta faced in her appeal for political asylum was that her story seemed both implausible and inconsistent to the immigration officials. Why would a prison guard accept a bribe and allow her to escape from a prison that no one left alive? If the authorities were after her, why did they kill her brother? How was she able to communicate with her mother? Why didn't she say in her first application that she had been raped? Margaretta was multiply stigmatized, already categorized according to hypervisibility categories as a fraud.

This much we could understand using a folkloristic understanding of repudiation and veneration. In principle, at least, nations offering asylum repudiate the violence people experience as a result of their political protest; they create the category of political asylum as a way of celebrating freedom and rescuing victims of persecution. However, to deserve this rescue, applicants are required (implicitly) to conform to the officials' expectations of what is normal. It's not normal to bribe your way out of jail, etc., etc. The asylum seekers' hypervisibility and the multiple stigmas they face can make them too unfamiliar, too unrecognizable to the immigration official's expected categories—and falling outside those categories fosters suspicion.

Asylum seekers' invisibility is produced not only by a choice to 'pass' and thus remain invisible in order to escape detention and deportation; it is also effected by legal processes that further stigmatize applicants by casting suspicion on 'illegal' acts they might have done to escape. Experiencing persecution as a result of engaging in political protest may not in itself be sufficient to qualify for asylum, especially for applicants who are suspected of 'criminal' behavior. Thus, applicants are multiply stigmatized by what they did and by what happened to them: they have bribed authorities; they have been raped by authorities who misused their power; they have, in many cases, broken the law during the course of their escape. Concepts of ethnocentrism are useful for acknowledging different cultural normalcies—differences that are difficult enough to explain in themselves. But asylum applicants are in the additionally challenging position of accounting for culturally specific modes of corruption and persecution. Veena Das and Arthur Kleinman suggest that the challenge for ethnographers is to attend to what they call "the local pitch" of survivors' stories to understand how they reconfigure themselves in response to devastating loss. In their description of Todeschini's study of the Japanese women who survived the bomb, they write:

The account by Todeschini of women as storytellers relates how women counter by various means the social death imposed upon them: they resist both the stigma and the cardboard heroic roles assigned to them. Listening to them as an ethnographic stance requires that we not only assign importance to their stories for the lessons Hiroshima or Nagasaki has to teach us in relation to the grand projects of world history, but also tune our ears to hear the more local pitch at which such women speak to establish a new morality for themselves. (2001, 11)

The "local pitch" is often unrecognizable to asylum officials. The appeal to pay attention to emic understandings is familiar to folklorists, but in this context, understanding is as much or more about the politics of visibility as it is about attending to local culture in context.

Although we began our research on political asylum a decade ago with the ethnographer's fundamental dependence on context as a means for clarifying discrepant interpretations, we have come to realize the limitations of attending to context as a means to address the problems in political asylum decisions. Initially, like others, we attempted to demonstrate how increased attention to different cultural contexts would prevent some of the mistakes immigration officials made so often in failing to recognize culturally different experiences of persecution and escape (Bohmer and Shuman 2008). We now realize the impossibility of attending to context as a source of greater understanding when the problem is the stigmatized vernacular of invisibility, that is, the failure to recognize that normalcy (upon which discussions of context depend) is a construction that is not even available in catastrophic situations. Lauren Berlant describes how the politics of invisibility and the stigmatized vernacular intersect in her recounting of Anita Hill's testimony before the US Senate:

A member of a stigmatized population testifies reluctantly to a hostile public the muted and anxious history of her imperiled citizenship. Her witnessing turns into a scene of teaching and an act of heroic pedagogy, in which the subordinated person feels compelled to recognize the privileged ones, to believe in their capacity to learn and to change; to trust their desire to not be inhuman; and trust their innocence of the degree to which their obliviousness has supported a system of political subjugation. These moments are acts of strange intimacy between subaltern peoples and those who have benefited by their subordination. (1997, 222)

Berlant's description could apply to the asylum seeker, though the stakes for the asylum seeker's "imperiled citizenship" involve deportation as well as hostility as possible outcomes, and the failure of the asylum seeker's testimony cannot be recuperated by lessons learned. However, Berlant is pointing to a profound connection between the loss of the ordinary and stigma. "Strange intimacy" describes the connection between those who are privileged to be normal and those who are excluded, an exclusion that perpetuates their connection, a connection that Goffman understood. In the context of exclusion, in which the familiar is so estranged as to be unattainable (because groups are deemed unqualified for it), making the familiar strange is a privilege.

Attention to cultural context fails because it is not possible to define the normal when the normal everyday has been completely replaced by routinized violence. In an essay on what he calls "cultural anesthesia," Allen Feldman describes a paper given by a Croatian folklorist about the "culture of fear in the former Yugoslavia." Feldman reports that the other ethnologists present at the conference were following Norbert Elias's argument "that modernization entails the progressive withdrawal of violence from everyday life in tandem with its increasing monopolization by the state" (Feldman 1994, 87). "Due to their adherence to Elias's perspective," he continued, "[they] had difficulty conceptualizing political violence as a routinized element of everyday life" (88). The ordinary escapes our (the ethnographer's, the asylum official's) attention (and requires defamiliarization) not only because it is routine (as phenomenologists have so importantly observed), but also because in stigmatizing situations (or in states of emergency) the ordinary operates as exclusionary. On these occasions, the ordinary can exclude some people by disqualifying them altogether.

Stigma and Visibility

Stigma works by assigning, legitimating, and disputing value, and it depends on making things visible, hypervisible, or invisible and then naturalizing those positions. In her essay "Food, Form, and Visibility: *Glub* and the Aesthetics of Everyday Life," Mieke Bal (2005) provides a good example of stigma as a negotiation of visibilities. Her larger collaboration with filmmaker Shahram Entekhabi on "the aesthetics of migration" profiles immigrants from the Middle East who purchase sunflower seeds in storefront shops and eat them in public spaces. The film *GLUB (Hearts)*, produced in 2003 and 2004, contrasts these subjects with gallery-going Germans who buy their sunflower seeds in boutique seed shops in Berlin. What is most evident in sunflower-seed eating is the trash left behind, the hulls of seeds spit out on the streets and sometimes consumed by birds. Entekhabi created a montage of people buying the seeds, eating them, and discarding the shells, a visual image that blurs categories of nature and culture, high and low culture, immigrant and native German (Entekhabi and Bal 2005).

The montage of people eating sunflower seeds in public creates a hypervisible image in which sunflower-seed-eating equals 'trash' equals 'immigrant creation of filth in public space'; by contrasting immigrants and Germans, the film also points to less visible social inequalities. Immigrants eat sunflower seeds in public and create trash; middle-class Germans eat sunflower seeds in public as a chic experience. The seeds themselves may be venerated as 'cuisine' even as the immigrants who imported the practice to Germany are repudiated. Mieke Bal describes the practice of eating seeds as a "hypervisible phenomenon of the near-invisible" (2005, 59). She argues that the more that particular immigrant cultural practices become "visible as such, the easier the host culture perceives them in terms of difference, a view that is always threatened [*sic*] to tip over into racism or its mitigated forms of exoticism and condescendence" (54).

Bal offers a model for understanding the role that visibility plays in the tipping point between difference and stigma. Gabriella Modan similarly explores the stigmatized vernacular in her discussion of filth in a multiethnic Washington, DC, neighborhood where she describes a "discursive type of spatial purification practice" (2007, 140). Real estate ads and public policies redefine the multiethnic neighborhood that appreciates the diversity of ethnic restaurants, but not ethnic residents. In these discourses, some dimensions of ethnicity are venerated because they represent diversity, and other dimensions (the residents themselves) are repudiated as sources of filth.

Barbara Kirshenblatt-Gimblett explains this paradox of simultaneous veneration and repudiation in terms of an asymmetry between the protection of universalized cultural assets and the protection of difference. In her essay "World Heritage and Cultural Economics," she notes "a paradoxical asymmetry between the diversity of those who produce cultural assets in the first place and the *humanity* to which those assets come to belong as world heritage" (2006,162). She describes diversity as working "centrifugally by generating cultural assets that can be universalized as world heritage, a process that expands the beneficiaries to encompass all of humanity." In contrast, "relativity works centripetally by invoking tolerance of difference to protect, insulate, and strengthen the capacities within individuals and communities to resist efforts to suppress their cultural practices, particularly in situations of religious and cultural conflict—a live and let live approach" (162).

Kirshenblatt-Gimblett defines heritage as "a mode of cultural production that gives the endangered or outmoded a second life as an exhibition of itself" (2006, 168). But what makes a mode of cultural production appear to be outmoded? What are the conditions of a repudiation that permits future veneration? Kirshenblatt-Gimblett argues that when the endangered or outmoded, which she also refers to as "neglected communities and traditions," are threatened with loss (which we could see as a lack of visibility or audibility), they become reconfigured as hypervisible (2006, 9). Importantly, the creation of the endangered and the creation of heritage are simultaneous; the stigma occurs with the hypervisibility.

These asymmetries produce and rely upon discourses of repudiation or stigma. The correction, the protection, or the recovery of culture proceeds quite differently depending on how a stigma is regarded. The relationship between veneration and repudiation is helpful for understanding the stigma that political asylum applicants face in their hearings with immigration officers. As a policy, political asylum depends on appreciation (not veneration) of the struggles people have faced and on the basic human right to be able to live without threat of torture or death due to political, religious, or cultural beliefs and/or practices. The policy venerates American ideals of freedom, and it can, by extension, at times celebrate the struggles of other peoples. This is complicated, of course, because not all asylum seekers share American values. Further compromising the ideal, many refugees who apply for political asylum are suspected (by officials and in media representations) of being fraudulent, of being economic migrants. And like economic migrants, asylum seekers are often repudiated as potentially (and illegitimately) taking resources from the host country (Westerman 1998).

The asymmetry that produces the possibility of venerating cultural practices but repudiating people depends in part on relations among the visible, the hypervisible, and the invisible. For example, Charles Briggs and Clara Mantini-Briggs (2003) discuss how the visibility of cholera participates in other asymmetries, especially between more and less valued groups. Their study demonstrates how indigenous and creole groups are seen differently. On the face of it, the difference "simply defines a local cultural economy as separate but equal," but distinguishing the two categories is actually "a cover for asymmetrical relationships, where one group is constructed as the complete version and the other is a partial and defective copy" (2003, 251).

Folklore and the Stigmatized Vernacular

The concept of the stigmatized vernacular represents a shift in the field of folklore and in the study of stigma, a shift from studying people at the margins to studying the conditions of marginalization. We note that the study of stigma in folklore is situated between discourses of veneration and repudiation. The folk, as conceptualized by nineteenth-century antiquarians and collectors, were a stigmatized group: they were the not-quite-modern peasants who were identifiable by their ways of dressing, talking, or behaving, or by their traditional (that is, not-quite-modern) cultural practices. However, if the people were stigmatized for their poverty, ruralness, or gender, their practices were venerated, at least by antiquarians and folklorists, as worth remembering and preserving.

The recognition of discourses of veneration and repudiation in folkloristics is, in part, a consequence of folklorists' interests in performance and everyday life. In an assessment of how folklorists have addressed diversity, Stephen Stern comments that pluralism in the academy opened up folklorists' subject matter even as it encouraged broader participation by scholars: "Previously existing marginal groups took center stage, with women, ethnics, and the disabled now leading the call to become legitimate areas for folkloristic investigation" (1991, 23). Later he adds,

> The folk no longer are any group of people who share beliefs, but a menagerie of opinions and interpretations whose differences are more important than similarities and who form coalitions rather than communities. . . . In place of a group with soul or communitas there are people with competing interests and natures who, in trying to make sense of the world, collide and collude to make social life a fractious enterprise. Such a debasement of a once cherished folk has led to what Henry Glassie (1983) calls a crisis in morality, fueled by a focus on the trivial rather than on the socially relevant. (1991, 25)

We suggest, however, that folklorists' insistence on "a once cherished folk" in fact perpetuates stigma.

Discourses of veneration, celebrations of the folk, even cultural relativism, are always intricately connected to discourses of repudiation. In a discussion of African American folklore studies, John Roberts critiques this veneration of the folk, arguing that such a stance obscures the complex diversity of African American cultural creativity (1993,164). Folklore is, to some degree, the study of the things people take pride in—and some cultural expressions are a response to stigma. Although one of the principles of ethnography is to study people on their own terms, not as repudiated, stigmatized, or discredited, ethnographers increasingly have been interested in the conditions of repudiation. Folklorists, in particular, are in a good position to understand discourses of repudiation and veneration in relation to each other and to the conditions that produce and sustain them. Folklorists can articulate how veneration, a seemingly positive gesture, can be a way of accepting people on our terms rather than expanding our concept of what counts as normal.[11] Identifying how veneration serves (or attempts to serve) as a corrective to repudiation is a good first step toward recognizing the folklorist's sometimes hidden agenda. In the form of empathy, veneration can be a dangerous corrective to stigma if it only serves the interests of the venerator (Shuman 2005).

Political asylum occupies a complex position in discourses of empathy and repute. Founded as a humanitarian gesture to offer safe haven to people whose own governments will not protect them, the political asylum hearing process has become a gatekeeping mechanism with the primary goal of weeding out fraudulent (i.e., economic) migrants. The distinction is between the loss of a livelihood (the fraudulent economic migrant masquerading as a political refugee) and the loss of a life. Both losses, in Giorgio Agamben's terms, result in the "bare life," the person without citizenship. Referring to Hannah Arendt's proposal that the condition of the refugee is "the paradigm of a new historical consciousness," Agamben suggests that statelessness is a central, rather than exceptional, condition of subjectivity (1995, 114). The refugee experiences exclusion from citizenship and other practices of ordinary life. This is a case of the ordinary (presumed to be normal) and the stigmatized mobilized in relation to, and defining, each other.

The stigmatized vernacular encompasses the practices of everyday, ordinary life that have been repudiated and that are sometimes legitimized, recognized, celebrated, or venerated. The dialectic of veneration and repudiation is part of a larger conversation about the dialectics of legitimation and contestation as interactive performances, whether in everyday life or in public policy.[12]

Notes

1. Davis describes normalcy as a hegemonic imperative that requires enforcement. "This normalcy must constantly be enforced in public venues (like the novel), must always be creating and bolstering its image by processing, comparing, constructing, deconstructing images of normalcy and the abnormal" (1995, 44) .

2. Here we propose a connection between Goffman's discussion of alienation resulting from a "discrepancy . . . between an individual's virtual and actual identity . . . [that] has the effect of cutting him off from society and from himself so that he stands a discredited person facing an unaccepting world" (1963, 57) and Viktor Shklovsky's discussions of estrangement. As Svetlana Boym points out in an article about Shklovsky's work, estrangement is not the same as the Marxist concept of alienation (2005, 588). We cannot review this complex concept here, but importantly, for our discussion, estrangement is not only a form of disengagement but also a source of the kind of awareness of difference (and then possible social change) that Goffman describes in *Stigma*.

3. One reviewer of this article commented on the fact that we refer to other scholars' work rather than to the people with whom we have established firsthand relationships. We could quote asylum applicants we have known who discuss issues such as routinized violence. However, whenever possible, and contrary to ethnographic practice, we substitute even third-hand observations in an attempt to avoid unnecessarily exploiting the individuals we know. As ethnographers, we believe we provide an important perspective for understanding political asylum, and we suggest that our research on political asylum is useful for disciplinary thinking about the stigmatized vernacular. However, our primary purpose in working with asylum seekers has been to help them to understand and prepare for the hearing process, not to collect examples for scholarship. Some individuals, including Margaretta, asked us to make their stories public.

4. Our explanation is based on our assessments of refusal letters produced by UK officials and on our work with asylum seekers over the past decade. The refusal letters provide an explanation for a denial, but we do not actually know how officials make their decisions. See the film *Well-Founded Fear* (Robertson and Camerini 2000) for personal accounts of US officials.

5. For a more thorough discussion of the political asylum process, see Bohmer and Shuman 2008.

6. "The commitment of the international community is to ensure to all persons the enjoyment of human rights, including the rights to life; to freedom from torture or cruel, inhuman, or degrading treatment or punishment; and to liberty and security of person. These and other rights are threatened when a refugee is returned to persecution or danger" (UN High Commissioner for Refugees 1997).

7. See Marilyn Ivy's discussion of trauma and the vanishing of the "imagined object of loss" (1995, 246).

8. The information was posted on the Prime Minister's Office website, http://www.spm.gov.cm. However, the following press release, issued November 30, 2006, is no longer available on the site: République Du Cameroun, "Press Release on Violent Student Strike at the University of Buea." http://www.spm.gov.cm/index_ac.php?param=accueil&r=r&d=11203&t=dss&lang=en (Accessed August 1, 2010).

9. Ellipses in this quote indicate pauses by the speaker.

10. In Bohmer and Shuman 2008 we document many cases of asylum officials' expectations about situations used to measure the credibility of applicants. See also Robertson and Camerini 2000 and Ranger 2008. These scholars and activists describe individual cases in depth, as we have, to document the complexity of officials' assessments of normalcy.

11. Katherine Borland (1991) attends to this issue in her discussion of her grandmother's refusal to be categorized as a feminist. Borland discusses the difficulty of representing people on their own terms.

12. This is one example of what John Brenkman calls for when he writes, "We must develop interpretive procedures which can account for the ways that the dialectic of legitimation and contestation internally structures expressive forms" (1987, 55).

References

Agamben, Giorgio. 1995. "We Refugees." Translated by Michael Rocke. *Symposium* 49 (2): 114–19.
———. 1998. *Homo Sacer.* Palo Alto, CA: Stanford University Press.
Bal, Mieke. 2005. "Food, Form, and Visibility: *Glub* and the Aesthetics of Everyday Life." *Postcolonial Studies* 8 (1): 51–73.
Berlant, Lauren. 1997. *The Queen of America Goes to Washington City: Essays on Sex and Citizenship.* Durham, NC: Duke University Press.
Blommaert, Jan. 2001. "Investigating Narrative Inequality: African Asylum Seekers' Stories in Belgium." *Discourse and Society* 12 (4): 413–49.
Bohmer, Carol, and Amy Shuman. 2004. "Representing Trauma: Political Asylum Narrative." *Journal of American Folklore* 117:394–414.

———. 2007. "Producing Epistemologies of Ignorance in the Political Asylum Application Process." *Identities: Global Studies in Culture and Power* 14 (5): 603–29.

———. 2008. *Rejecting Refugees: Political Asylum in the 21st Century.* New York: Routledge.

———. 2010. "Contradictory Discourses of Protection and Control in Transnational Asylum Law." *Journal of Legal Anthropology* 1 (2): 212–29.

Borland, Katherine. 1991. "'That's Not What I Said': Interpretive Conflict in Oral Narrative Research." In *Women's Words: The Feminist Practice of Oral History,* edited by Shawna Gluck and Daphne Patai, 63–75. New York: Routledge.

Boym, Svetlana. 2005. "Poetics and Politics of Estrangement: Victor Shklovsky and Hannah Arendt." *Poetics Today* 26 (4): 581–611.

Brenkman, John. 1987. *Culture and Domination.* Ithaca, NY: Cornell University Press.

Briggs, Charles, and Clara Mantini-Briggs. 2003. *Stories in a Time of Cholera: Racial Profiling during a Medical Nightmare.* Berkeley and Los Angeles: University of California Press.

Campbell, Nancy. 2004. "Technologies of Suspicion: Coercion and Compassion in Post-Disciplinary Surveillance Regimes." *Surveillance and Society* 2 (1): 78–92.

Caruth, Cathy. 1995. "An Interview with Robert Jay Lifton." In *Trauma: Explorations in Memory,* edited by Cathy Caruth, 128–46. Baltimore, MD: Johns Hopkins University Press.

Culbertson, Roberta. 1995. "Embodied Memory, Transcendence, and Telling: Recounting Trauma, Re-establishing the Self." *New Literary History* 26:169–95.

Das, Veena. 2007. *Life and Words: Violence and the Descent into the Ordinary.* Berkeley and Los Angeles: University of California Press.

Das, Veena, and Arthur Kleinman. 2001. *Remaking a World: Violence, Social Suffering, and Recovery.* Berkeley and Los Angeles: University of California Press.

Davis, Lennard. 1995. *Enforcing Normalcy.* London: Verso.

———. 2006. "Constructing Normalcy: The Bell Curve, the Novel, and the Invention of the Disabled Body in the Nineteenth Century." In *The Disability Studies Reader,* edited by Lennard Davis, 3–16. New York: Routledge.

Dembour, Marie-Bénédicte. 1996. "Human Rights Talk and Anthropological Ambivalence: The Particular Contexts of Universal Claims." In *Inside and Outside The Law: Anthropological Studies of Authority and Ambiguity,* edited by Olivia Harris, 19–40. London: Routledge.

Einhorn, Bruce J. 2009. "Consistency, Credibility, and Culture." In *Refugee Roulette: Disparities in Asylum Adjudication and Proposals for Reform,* edited by Jaya Ramji-Nogales, Andrew I. Schoenholtz, and Philip G. Schrag, 187–201. New York: NYU Press.

Entekhabi, Shahram, and Mieke Bal. 2005. *GLUB (Hearts).* Installation brochure. Zug, Switzerland: Fine Arts Unternehmen www.fineartsunternehmen.com/film/brochures/glub.pdf.

Feldman, Allen. 1994. "From Desert Storm to Rodney King via ex-Yugoslavia: On Cultural Anaesthesia." In *The Senses Still: Perception and Memory As Material Culture in Modernity,* edited by C. Nadia Serematakis, 87–107. Chicago, IL: University of Chicago Press.

Freire, Paulo. 1974. *Pedagogy of the Oppressed.* Translated by M. B. Ramos. New York: Seabury Press. Original work published in 1968.

Goffman, Erving. 1963. *Stigma: Notes on the Management of Spoiled Identity.* Englewood Cliffs, NJ: Prentice Hall.

Herskovits, Melville. 1972. *Cultural Relativism: Perspectives in Cultural Pluralism.* New York: Random House.

Herzfeld, Michael. 2005. "Minding the Gap: Toward a Historical Poetics of Estrangement." *Poetics Today* 26 (4): 613–36.

Ivy, Marilyn. 1995. *Discourses of the Vanishing: Modernity, Phantasm, Japan.* Chicago: University of Chicago Press.

Jackson, Michael. 2002. *The Politics of Storytelling: Violence, Transgression, and Intersubjectivity.* Copenhagen: Museum Tusculanum Press.

Jacquemet, Marco. 1996. *Credibility in Court: Communicative Practices in the Camorra Trials.* Cambridge: Cambridge University Press.

Khanna, Ranjana. 2006. "Asylum." *Texas International Law Journal* 41 (3): 471–90.

Kirshenblatt-Gimblett, Barbara. 2006. "World Heritage and Cultural Economics." In *Museum Frictions: Public Cultures/Global Transformations,* edited by Ivan Karp, Corinne A. Kratz, Lynn Szwaja, and Tomas Ybarra-Frausto, 161–202. Durham, NC: Duke University Press.

Lewis, Rachel. 2012. "Lesbian Asylum Narratives and the Cultural Politics of Desire and Belonging." Paper presented at the Transnational Sexualities and Human Rights Faculty Workshop, University of Connecticut, April 20.

Miggiano, Luca. 2009. "States of Exception: Securitisation and Irregular Migration in the Mediterranean." Research Paper 177, New Issues in Refugee Research Series. United Nations High Commissioner for Refugees, Policy Development and Evaluation Service Working Papers. http://www.unhcr.org/4b167a5a9.html.

Modan, Gabriella. 2007. *Turf Wars: Discourse, Diversity, and the Politics of Place.* Oxford: Blackwell.

New York Times. 1999. "Official Charged with Taking Bribes to Grant Immigrants Political Asylum." April 24. http://www.nytimes.com/1999/04/24/nyregion/official-charged-with-taking-bribes-to-grant-immigrants-political-asylum.html.

Ramji-Nogales, Jaya, Andrew I. Schoenholtz, and Philip G. Schrag. 2009. *Refugee Roulette: Disparities in Asylum Adjudication and Proposals for Reform.* New York: NYU Press.

Ranger, Terence. 2008. "The Narratives and Counter-Narratives of Zimbabwean Asylum: Female Voices." In *Connecting Cultures,* edited by Emma Bainbridge, 19–36. New York: Routledge.

Renteln, Alison Dundes. 1988. "Relativism and the Search for Human Rights." *American Anthropologist* 90 (1): 56–72.

Roberts, John W. 1993. "African American Diversity and the Study of Folklore." *Western Folklore* 52 (2/4): 157–71.

Robertson, Shari, and Michaeli Camerini, directors. 2000. *Well-Founded Fear.* DVD. New York: The Epidavros Project.

Schuster, Liza. 2003. *The Use and Abuse of Asylum in Britain and Germany.* London: Routledge.

Shuman, Amy. 2005. *Other People's Stories: Entitlement Claims and the Critique of Empathy.* Urbana: University of Illinois Press.

Silverman, Carol. 2012. *Romani Routes: Cultural Politics and Balkan Music in Diaspora.* Oxford: Oxford University Press.

Stern, Stephen. 1991. "The Influence of Diversity on Folklore Studies in the Decades of the 1980s and '90s." *Western Folklore* 50 (1): 21–7.

Terretta, Meredith. 2012. "Expert Testimony and the (A)political: Changing Roles for Expert Witnesses in African and Global Politics since the 1950s." Paper presented at the Conable Conference on Political Asylum, April 19, Rochester Institute of Technology, Rochester, New York, USA.

UN High Commissioner for Refugees. 1997. "UNHCR Note on the Principle of Non-Refoulement." November. http://www.unhcr.org/refworld/docid/438c6d972.html.

Welsch, Roger. 2009. "Confessions of a Wannabe: When the Prime Directive Backfires." Invited Plenary Address presented at the Annual Meeting of the American Folklore Society, October 22, in Boise, Idaho, USA.

Westerman, William. 1998. "Central American Refugee Testimonies and Performed Life Histories in the Sanctuary Movement." In *The Oral History Reader,* edited by Robert Perks and Alistair Thomson, 167–81. London: Routledge.

AMY SHUMAN is Professor of Folklore at The Ohio State University. Her publications include *Storytelling Rights: The Uses of Oral and Written Texts by Urban Adolescents* (2006), *Other People's Stories: Entitlement Claims and the Critique of Empathy* (2010), and, with Carol Bohmer, *Rejecting Refugees: Political Asylum in the 21st Century* (2008).

CAROL BOHMER is a lawyer and sociologist who is currently a Visiting Scholar in the Government Department at Dartmouth College and a Teaching Fellow in the War Studies Department at King's College London. She has published articles about asylum, domestic violence, rape, and divorce. With Amy Shuman, she published *Rejecting Refugees: Asylum in the Twenty-First Century* (2008).

Index

Adorno, Theodor, 9
Agamben, Giorgio, 98, 112–13
AIDS/HIV, 71–73, 83
Alcoff, Linda, 85
American Association of University Women (AAUW), 14
American Folklore Society, 2, 93
Anagnostu, Georgios, 9
architecture, 4, 5, 37n16
Arendt, Hannah, 113
asylum. *See* political asylum
authenticity, 9, 65n20, 73

Babcock, Barbara, 64n3
Bamberg, Michael G. W., 8
barbarism, 2, 6
Bateson, Gregory, 44
Bauman, Richard, 44, 64n3
Behar, Ruth, 11n1
Benedict, Ruth, 94
Bennett, Gillian, 7
Berger, Harris M., 43, 64n3
Berlant, Lauren, 107–8
Berry, Wendell, 21, 25, 36n6
Bock, Sheila, 8
Bohmer, Carol, 6–7, 75, 77, 83, 94–95, 97, 99–101, 104–5, 107, 114n10
Bond, Jerry, 24
Bond, Kathleen, 24
Borland, Katherine, 114n11
Bourgois, Philippe, 83
Boym, Svetlana, 113n2
Brenkman, John, 114n12
Briggs, Charles, 9, 44, 61–62, 111

Brison, Susan, 78, 86n6
Brooks, Peter, 82
Burke, Kenneth, 18

Cameroon, 91, 95–102. *See also* political asylum
Campbell, Nancy, 105
Capps, Lisa, 7, 75
Cartwright, Christine, 7
Caruth, Cathy, 104
Clifford, James, 73–74
conversation analysis, 15
creole, 5, 9, 11
Culbertson, Roberta, 76
cultural relativism, 90, 92–94, 112

dairy farming, 34–35, 36n2, 38n25
Dar es Salaam U.S. Embassy bombings, 78–79
Das, Veena, 48, 105–7
Davis, Lennard, 93, 113n1
Dégh, Linda, 36n5
Del Negro, Giovanna P., 43, 64n3
devaluation, 48, 62–63, 80–81, 92
diabetes-related stigma, 2, 6, 43–64, 65n20; and blame, 46–47; fieldwork, 43–44, 49–50, 60–62; gestational diabetes, 64n4; and race, 46–61, 65n16; and reflexivity, 43–44, 49–51, 60–63; type 1 and type 2 diabetes, 44–46
disassociation, 71, 77, 79–80
discourse: cultural discourse, 6, 43–45, 54–59, 63; of heritage, 5–6, 14–29, 32, 34–35, 38n22; and hierarchies of value, 9; indirect discourse, 54–55; metadiscursive practices, 61, 65n20;

Printed and bound by CPI Group (UK) Ltd, Croydon, CR0 4YY

13/04/2025

14656543-0002